BRING RAIN

Helping Humanity in Crisis

SARAH DAWN PETRIN

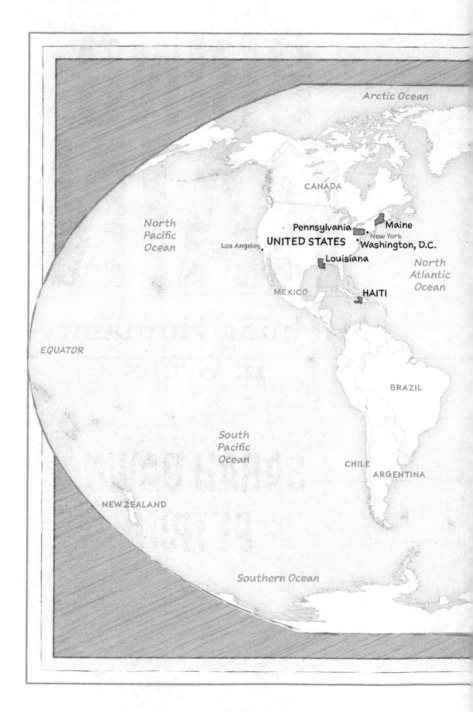

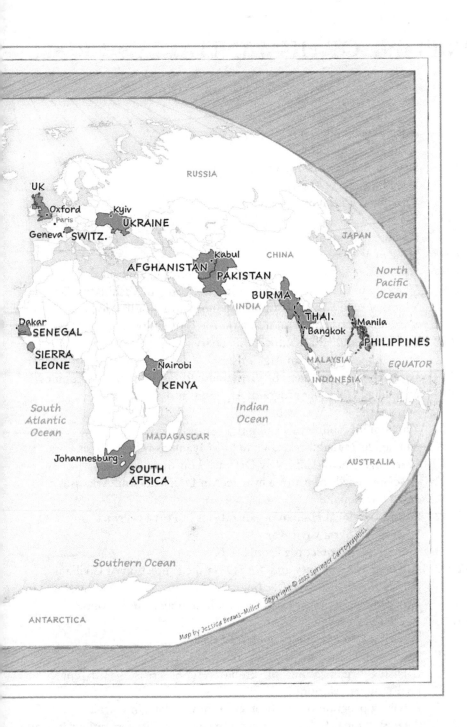

RUSSIA

UK
Oxford
Paris
Geneva   SWITZ.
Kyiv
UKRAINE

JAPAN
CHINA

Kabul
AFGHANISTAN   PAKISTAN
INDIA

North
Pacific
Ocean

BURMA
THAI.
Bangkok
Manila
PHILIPPINES
MALAYSIA
EQUATOR
INDONESIA

Dakar
SENEGAL

SIERRA
LEONE

Nairobi
KENYA

South
Atlantic
Ocean

MADAGASCAR

Indian
Ocean

AUSTRALIA

Johannesburg
SOUTH
AFRICA

Southern Ocean

ANTARCTICA

Map by Jessica Brams-Miller   Copyright © 2020 Springer Cartographics

TIMELINE OF HUMANITARIAN CRISES
In this book (1976–2020)

1976	Born during a drought in Mumias, Kenya
1985	Ethiopia Famine Relief
1990–1994	Student in High School, literacy volunteer
1992	Somalia Refugee Crisis
1992	Building a school in Kisumu, Kenya
1992–1994	War in the Former Yugoslavia
1994	Rwandan Genocide
1994–1998	Student at Gordon College
1996–1997	Conducting census of Mauritanian Refugees in Senegal
1998–1999	Working in the Senate, U.S. Capitol shooting in Washington D.C.
1999–2000	Working with World Vision in Johannesburg, South Africa
2001	September 11th terrorist attack on the United States
2001–2002	Graduate Student at Oxford University
2001	Start of the U.S. War in Afghanistan
2002–2004	Facilitating resettlement of Vietnamese Refugees in the Philippines
2002–2003	Managing UN relief program, Afghanistan-Pakistan border
2003	Start of the U.S. War in Iraq
2004	Tsunami hits southern Thailand
2005	Managing Tsunami relief, Thailand-Myanmar refugee crisis
2005	Hurricane Katrina hits New Orleans, Louisiana
2005–2006	Assessing needs of Katrina evacuees in Louisiana and Arkansas
2010	Haiti Earthquake
2010–2012	Supporting local Haitian organizations in Port-au-Prince
2011	Start of the Syria Civil War
2012	Founding of Protect the People (PTP)
2012–2018	Advising U.S. military and NATO on the Protection of Civilians
2014	Russia invades Eastern Ukraine
2015	Global Refugee Crisis leads to 1 million arrivals in Europe
2013–2016	Ebola Outbreak in West Africa
2016	Advising Ebola response in Sierra Leone
2016–2017	Managing Hurricane Matthew relief in Haiti
2017	Advising organizations on global refugee crisis, health epidemics, civil-military relations
2018	Advising program on the Protection of Civilians in Ukraine
2019	Analyst at the U.S. Army Peacekeeping and Stability Operations Institute
2020	Global Coronavirus Pandemic

EARLY PRAISE FOR BRING RAIN

"Reading this book is like sitting and having a friendly and frank conversation with Sarah herself where she fills you in on the lessons she's learned during her fascinating and varied career."

> —Anne C. Richard, former Assistant Secretary of State
> for Population, Refugees and Migration (PRM) at U.S.
> Department of State

"This book describes the power and paradox of humanitarian service. It changes us—perhaps even more than we change others. We become learners as much as we are teachers. We become beneficiaries as much as we are aid workers. We learn from local wisdom as much as we bring solutions to global problems. At its core, the most effective humanitarian work is about deep engagement with others that leads to mutual transformation."

> —Daryl Byler, Development Director, DC Bar Foundation
> and former Executive Director, Eastern Mennonite
> University's Center for Justice and Peacebuilding

"Drawing on her work in communities affected by natural disasters, refugee crises, and conflict, Petrin offers both a call to action and a blueprint for meaningful engagement in our complex world."

> —Dr. Gary Kirk, Director of the Center for Civic
> Engagement at Dickinson College

"This is an excellent book for any person young or old who is contemplating working as a humanitarian in the field or a headquarters. The book is packed with personal examples of someone who has lived the life over 20 years. The book holds your attention with examples of real-life dilemmas and makes you want to jump in the fray to help."
—*Colonel Brian Foster (Ret.), U.S. Army*

"In this book, readers will see their shared story in the face of crisis and learn hands-on ways to respond to the needs around them. Because while the world does need each one of us, Sarah shows us that we also really need the world."
—*Lisa-Jo Baker, bestselling author of Never Unfriended and Cohost of the Out of the Ordinary Podcast*

"This book helps me to be a better leader, educator, and person."
—*Jennifer Tynan-Tyrrell, Program Coordinator at Yellow Breeches Educational Center*

"Sarah shows us that humanitarian action can start at your front door or take you across the globe; this book emphasizes the importance of thoughtful and critical reflection for those who pursue humanitarian action as a career and highlights the challenges and opportunities such a life can bring."
—*Jacob Kurtzer, Interim Director of the Humanitarian Agenda, Center for Strategic and International Studies (CSIS)*

ADVANCE PRAISE FOR BRING RAIN

"This book is a testament to the simple but consequential principle of humanity. The idea that the rights and well-being of individuals affected by humanitarian crisis—wherever they might occur—must command the attention of humankind is pervasive in Sarah Petrin's book. The book also stands for the proposition that each of us can—indeed must—serve this noble principle of humanity no matter what specific professional path we ultimately choose to travel."
—*Eric Schwartz, President of Refugees International and former Dean, Hubert H. Humphrey School of Public Affairs, University of Minnesota*

"In a broken world, many individuals wonder if there is hope for humanity and how to help those who are hurting. *Bring Rain* addresses those concerns, as well as many others, as Sarah demonstrates how to be an agent of change through her life stories."
—*Hannah Domaracki, student at Messiah College*

"Sarah has written a solid and readable primer on the world of international humanitarian assistance based on her decades of experience in this field. It will serve as a useful tool for anybody contemplating a career devoted to assisting populations affected by crisis."
—*Doug Mercado, Visiting Lecturer, Princeton University*

"This book is heartfelt, informative, moving, and educational."
—*Lindsay Musser Hough, Principal at Deloitte Consulting and Author of A Woman's Framework for a Successful Career and Life*

BRING RAIN

Helping Humanity
in Crisis

SARAH DAWN
PETRIN

CONTENTS

Dear Reader,

As you will see from reading this book, every crisis presents us with both a challenge and an opportunity. Right now, whether we see our challenges as opportunities is up to each of us.

When I first started writing this book, the world was a different place. Little did I know it then, that a virus called COVID-19 would spread throughout the globe and dramatically change our lives.

The virus has brought us all closer to the idea that what happens in a seemingly far-off corner of the world can touch us all. The pandemic has challenged us to think about the vulnerable, to protect one another from getting sick, and to learn about the science of global health. For many, the virus has brought about tremendous loss, grieving loved ones, destroying livelihoods, and hurting businesses.

Yet, the virus offers us what every crisis does—an opportunity to reflect and rebuild. This ability to recover from devastating loss comes from within. Many involved in relief work call this trait "resilience," the ability to recover from multiple shocks.

The global pandemic has shown us that we can weather this storm, and the next one, and the one after that. We already know the danger ahead—the climate crisis—which begs us to take better care of our planet and the people within it. The work ahead is yours to do. This book will give you the practical tips you need to get going and I hope my personal stories will inspire you to make a difference.

Be on your way, find your own path, and do good.

Godspeed,
Sarah

DEDICATION

This book is dedicated to the "doers," the "helpers," and people who care.

It is dedicated to the modern-day miracle workers, the humanitarians, who put their own lives on the line to save others.

Aid workers perform miracles every day. They secure food stockpiles before famine arrives, they land planes where there are no runways, they tap water when the well has run dry, they rescue children from the underground, they set prisoners free. They find money in places when all the resources in the world have run out. They are simply amazing, *the best of the best.*

These aid workers come from different backgrounds and have varying beliefs. Yet, they all share a faith in humanity. They believe in the power of extending goodwill to all people simply because they are human beings. They see the promise of a better world and they pursue it.

This book is dedicated to them, and to those of you who will join them in the days ahead. You don't have to be a saint or a superhero to save lives. Whether you are traveling afar or staying close to home, you only have to see the needs around you and be ready to respond.

PROLOGUE

The Call

There I was, sitting by myself at John F. Kennedy airport in New York City when I got the call. And somehow, I knew that my whole life after that moment hung in the balance.

I was fresh off the plane from Nairobi, Kenya and was waiting for a connecting flight to take me home to Maine when an overwhelming feeling washed over me. People rushed by me in every direction, hurrying to get to their destination. I wondered,

Where am I really meant to be?

I didn't want to go home. It was time to do something else, to go somewhere else. I wanted to help the refugees I saw, but what could I do? I was only fifteen years old.

I found a quiet corner where I could gather my thoughts. I wasn't ready to go home yet, but I wasn't sure where else I was going. The world was so big, and there was so much to explore. The team in Kenya built the foundation for a school, but we didn't finish anything. Then, I heard an almost audible whisper.

You will go to many people and many places.

I looked all around. There was no one near me. I looked around some more, then I heard it again.

You will go to many people and many places. You will help many people.

The voice came from deep within my spirit. I knew what it said was true, that this was the beginning of a life-long call to serve people in need.

Yes, I thought, *I want to go. I want to go now.*

*Wherever that voice was telling me to go, I wanted to go there **right away**. I didn't want to get on the plane home. Then, I thought of my Mom. She would miss me if I didn't come back. Plus, I had to finish high school.*

I got on the plane and flew home to Maine.

When you first sense a call to help others, the world seems to open up before you. This awareness may come from the first time you volunteer in a new area or the first time you travel abroad. There are so many needs, it's hard to know where to start.

That is why I'm going to tell you an important lesson at the outset: The best gift you can give the world is to give yourself. You are a unique person with skills and experiences to share with others. You are one of a kind; there is no one like you.

You have the compassion to help and the determination to do something. How, then, can you best use the skills you've been given? Knowing how, when, and where to go is a critical first step to applying yourself.

Finding Your Mission

I want you to have a great life, no matter where you come from, what you do for work, or where you live. Helping humanity is about seeing the worth and dignity of all people.

This book will show you the way to lead a meaningful life by helping people.

This book will also give you a series of steps to help you determine how you are uniquely suited to make a difference. It will take you on a journey from wanting to help to actually going out and acting. Like me, you may face obstacles and setbacks, but I will show you how to surmount every one of them.

This book will give you what it takes to be a helper. You are going to need steadfast determination and the confidence that everything you do—no matter how seemingly small—is part of the bigger picture of human progress.

I am sharing my experiences to embolden you, to help you recognize that the world needs you, and to assure you that you have been called to a high and worthwhile purpose.

In the chapters ahead, I'll show you how to go from knowing that something needs to be done to becoming the person who springs into action. And so, I'll tell you now:

The first step to living a life of service is leaving your comfort zone.

For some of us, that also means leaving home. Whether you go to a new neighborhood or a different country, stepping out from where you are now will lead you to new opportunities. Being able to leave your comfort zone is something that needs to be understood before you go anywhere, and we will revisit this shortly.

Once I decided to pursue humanitarian work, I knew I wasn't going to live a normal life—the kind of normal life where you finish school, get a job, find a spouse, buy a house, have kids, and settle down. If I was going to serve refugees, I would be traveling and living overseas. I would have to "settle down" later.

I knew this was true when I returned home to Maine for summer break after studying abroad in Senegal where I worked with refugees on the border of Mauritania. Being a humanitarian was going to demand more of me than a career choice— it was an altogether different lifestyle that would determine where I lived, how much money I would make, and who I would eventually settle down with to have a family of my own.

I can remember standing at the top of the Eastern Promenade in Portland, Maine. I could see across Casco Bay with its deep blue waters graced by ferry lines taking passengers to the nearby islands. This idyllic, peaceful place was my home. *Why would I ever want to leave?*

Maine is one of the most beautiful states in the country. Surrounded by the Atlantic Ocean on its right flank and bordered by the state of New Hampshire to its left, Maine is known for its pine green wilderness and ruby red lobsters. It is a vacationland to seasonal visitors who flock to its islands for summer vacations. You can feel the serenity in the sea salt air as it blows across your face. It's no wonder the state motto is *"The Way Life Should Be."*

Here I was, on a beautiful summer day, knowing that simply being from Maine was a luxury. But staring out at the serene ocean, I was anything but calm on the inside. My mind drifted back to being in refugee camps in the desert. Only a few weeks before, I was with refugees from Mauritania, some of whom were dying from cholera.

Wouldn't life be easier, I thought, *if I married a nice boy from Maine and stayed here?* I had a boyfriend through my last years of high school. He wanted to build a house next door to his parents. He couldn't understand my desire to help people in far-off places. He also didn't know what it really required. He eventually had a family and achieved the American dream.

But I knew that helping refugees meant sacrificing things and people that could limit my opportunities. I stood staring at the ocean—knowing that the course I was choosing meant giving up winters warming by a cozy fire, family dinners, and summers playing in the waves along Maine's rocky coast. I wasn't sure when I would find a partner and have children, but I knew that when I did, I wanted them to be part of my vision to help humanity.

This is an important point for you to remember:

Once you know what you are called to do, don't let anyone or anything get in the way. Other people may have a different agenda for your life, distractions will come your way, and alternatives will present themselves. Don't get distracted— stay the course. Live the life you are meant to live.

Get a Good Education

Another thing that's required to help humanity, in addition to getting out of your comfort zone, is to get a good education. A good education is the foundation of a professional, humanitarian career. Many students pursuing an international career start with an undergraduate degree in International Relations, then specialize in a particular field for their master's degree. For example, as an undergraduate student at Gordon College, I pursued a Bachelor of Arts (BA) in International Relations. I also earned a degree in French by taking all the required language courses and received a Pike Scholar award, which allowed me to design a major in African Studies.

Thus, I graduated with a degree in three majors: International Relations, French, and African Studies. This is somewhat unusual, but I received extra credit from Advanced Placement (AP) courses in high school by taking summer classes at Georgetown University in Washington, D.C. and by studying abroad for a semester in West Africa. You might think that I was an overachiever, but I didn't set out to complete three majors. It happened by mak-ing the most of every opportunity. While you are a student, you have a suite of people around you to help you learn. Make the most of every opportunity you have for experiential learning.

Selecting a good degree program matters, but numerous majors and types of degrees are options for pursuing humani-tarian work. You can pursue political science or business admin-istration and take coursework in international relations. One particular survey of humanitarian workers indicated that regard-less of the degree, aid workers did not feel that their education prepared them for the field.[1] This is because the work is complex and varied in nature, with a lot of "on the job" training. What matters most is how you use your education to develop the skills and knowledge you need to thrive in the aid sector.

Eventually, as you pursue specific jobs, your unique skill set will matter more than your educational background. This skill set includes language skills and experience working abroad. To get experience, you can start by doing short-term service proj-ects or study abroad programs with more experiential learning objectives. For example, I chose to study in Senegal, West Africa because the regional bureau for the UN High Commissioner

---

[1]Reis, Chris and Bernath, Tania. *Becoming an International Humanitarian Aid Worker*, Cambridge, Butterworth-Heinemann of Elsevier, 2017.

for Refugees was located there, and the program included an internship or independent study option with course credit.

Many undergraduates also look to do internships or fellowships with international organizations. For some people in the United States, the Peace Corps is also a good way to get international experience and language skills. Peace Corps volunteers also benefit from a wide network of returned volunteers who support those coming out of their assignments with job placement and career counseling services.

However, Peace Corps service is not for everyone. Although the model is changing, being placed in a remote village is not always the best way to understand the local culture. This is particularly true if you want to work with refugees or migrants who are on the move. Also, female volunteers who are placed in traditional cultural settings can experience enormous pressure to marry a local partner while serving. In my opinion, urban placements in regional centers or towns are more desirable, since these areas are less isolated and tend to have a broader social network. Whatever type of learning experience you pursue, make sure that you are in a safe place where you can highlight what you learned and how you served the community.

While having an undergraduate education is foundational, many humanitarians pursue graduate work in a specialized area. For example, I did my Master's in Forced Migration from the Refugee Studies Center at Oxford University in the United Kingdom. You may also want to consider a specialized degree in Anthropology, Communications, Engineering, Finance, Logistics, Medicine, Public Health, Public Policy, International Law, Environmental Studies, Gender Studies, and Regional Studies that emphasize a particular geographic area or sector.

Whatever course of education you pursue, it's important to remember that having experience in the field is often considered more important than education. Many entry-level positions available are within non-governmental organizations that will also provide you with on-the-job training and field experience.

If you only have education but no experience, you are more likely to have a desk job that focuses on administration, analysis, policy, or research. You will need a combination of education and experience, with specialized training and certificates in specific skills like grant writing or program management, to meet the criteria for more advanced positions in this line of work.

When I finished college, I wanted to go abroad right away. But I needed more work experience. I also realized that learning how to advocate for better policies to help people was an important skill I wanted to develop.

I decided to move to Washington, D.C. and work for Senator Olympia J. Snowe from Maine. Strange to think that someone who was desperate to work overseas would take a detour to Washington, but my sense of calling led me there.

As it turned out, Washington was a home away from home for someone like me. Having been born overseas in Kenya, I felt connected to other people around the world from a young age. When I got my first phone, a baby blue land line with a rotary dial, I immediately wanted to call people in other countries. I didn't know anyone living overseas at the time, but I wanted to reach out and make friends with people from different backgrounds.

In the nation's Capital, you find representatives from every state. Within a few square miles, you find embassies with representatives from every country. It's a place full of diversity with new people always moving into the city for work.

Specifically, I was looking to work for an international organization that would send me overseas. Back in Maine, there were a few nonprofit organizations helping refugees settle into the state and trade groups working on international business opportunities. I was looking for work that would bring systemic changes to how society cares for vulnerable people, especially those affected by war and disasters. At least I thought that was what I wanted. But was that just an idealistic thought?

Working in the Senate was exciting every day. Senator Snowe served on the powerful Armed Services Committee and was a moderate. She had strong views about making the government work for the people, making health care affordable, and improving the lives of women at home and abroad. In her office, there was a new situation to respond to every few hours, a new legislative proposal that needed to be analyzed, or a new event in the press that required talking points.

I worked my way up from being a front office receptionist to serving as a legislative correspondent, which meant I wrote responses to letters that the Senator received in the mail. I also wrote talking points for media interviews, speeches, and hearing testimony on a wide range of topical issues. Even though I was a young staffer, I did interesting things like give private tours of the Capitol Building to visitors from Maine.

On one ordinary day, I was asked to give a tour of the Capitol to a group of journalists from my home state.

"This is a VIP tour; these journalists are from the largest paper in Maine," the Chief of Staff of the office told me. "You never know," he said jokingly, "*one day they could write a story about you.*"

Little did he know, it would hardly be a normal tour.

As my group entered the basement of the rotunda, the center of the Capitol building, my group was looking at the different displays, when an active shooter appeared out of nowhere, storming through the metal detectors.

I heard a loud *bang* that sounded like something heavy hit the concrete, but the second shot was unmistakable. **We were under fire.**

"Take cover!" I shouted to my group. "This way!" I ushered my group into a women's bathroom about 10 feet away, then closed the door. I looked around to see; did I have everyone with me? I started to count the number of people with me, when one of the journalists came up to me, panicking.

"My wife and my baby—they didn't make it in. I'm going out to find them," he said, and he started to push past me.

"No," I told him forcibly as I barricaded the door with my body. As much as he wanted to find his family, I had to stop him from opening the door. There was more gunfire outside. Whatever was going on, it was far from over. I told him empathetically,

"We don't know how many shooters are out there. But I can hear the police outside. We have to wait for instructions." I prayed that the woman and child found cover elsewhere.

When the police knocked on the door of the bathroom, they were ready to escort us out of the building. We quickly exited the area, not knowing what had really happened. When we got back to the front office, the woman and the baby were waiting for us. Just as I prayed, someone—a policeman—had ushered them to another safe location when the shots rang out. It was a tearful, happy reunion.

To finish the story, we watched the office television to learn what happened. A lone shooter, a mentally unstable man, stormed the security entrance to the capital. He killed two capitol police officers before he was also killed by the police.

The next day, I was on the front page of *Portland Press Herald* under the headline:

YOUNG STAFFER KEEPS EVERYONE CALM

The journalists did tell my story, of how I took charge, keeping everyone calm as I ushered the group to safety in the nearest shelter, a women's bathroom.

More to the point, this strange and harrowing event made me decide what kind of life I would lead: *I would answer the call to save lives no matter where I was in the world, no matter the difficulty or circumstance.*

That was an extraordinary day in the office, but there were also plenty of ordinary ones. After all, it was my job to answer the mail. Yet sometimes even the most mundane days presented opportunities to make a difference—which also became an important lesson about following your calling.

Every day, I saw an older woman named Gladys, a janitor who worked hard, cleaning bathrooms in the Senate buildings. One day she appeared tired and discouraged. I heard her tell another colleague that she felt invisible. She wondered out loud, *"What good is all my hard work doing?"*

Immediately, I asked myself, *"On ordinary days that seem to drag on, what can I do?"* An idea came to me. Every day I used the power of the pen to put the Senator's signature on all kinds of requests. I thought, what if I wrote a letter from the Senator recognizing Gladys and all her hard work? That might lift her spirits. I drafted the letter, and the Senator agreed to send it to the head of cleaning services.

Days later, Gladys came to the office asking who had written the letter. When I met her, she was overjoyed to the point of tears. "Because of this letter, I got a pay raise!"

I tried to deflect her enthusiasm. "You deserved the raise. You're a hard worker."

"You don't understand," she insisted. "No one in my department has ever received a letter from a Member of Congress."

From that day on, Gladys held her head up a bit higher.

I'll never forget what that taught me:

You can help people no matter where you are or what position you are in, as long as you look out for the needs of others and take action.

The impact that one letter made on Gladys, and keeping people calm during the Capitol shooting, taught me a valuable lesson. You don't have to be in a position of authority to save a life or impact one. You just have to be willing to respond, each and every day, when the situation presents itself. *Look around you, see where there is a need, and be ready to respond.*

Be Ready to Go

When the time came for me to leave Washington, it was through someone who wanted to help me. A leader in a large nongovernmental organization (NGO), whom I met in Senegal, West Africa had just moved to Washington, D.C. He asked me to help him make sense of how Capitol Hill worked. We met regularly over lunch to talk about the news of the day. One day, he asked me.

"If you could go anywhere in the world, where would it be?"

"I want to go anywhere I can learn how to be the best relief worker," I said.

I want to work with the best team.

He knew just the place. In South Africa, there was a global, troubleshooting team that responded to any major event in the world within 24 hours.

"This team just came out of Rwanda and Bosnia," he said. "They are the best. The organization has decided to turn its global relief group into a technical services team that will train regional response teams. They need support to collect best practices and conduct trainings. Your job will be to ensure that they have the latest information on food aid, child protection, and relief standards. Then, you will use that information to train local responders all over the world."

"I'm ready to go," I said, eagerly.

A month later, I was on a plane to Johannesburg, South Africa, going overseas to be closer to the frontlines of humanitarian action. I was "officially" on my way. Working in South Africa was my first professional assignment in the field. Although I wanted to work directly with refugee populations, I knew my assignment would be in a regional office supporting missions from afar. *I needed to learn not only how to assist people in need, but how to manage programs which involved getting to know the back end of relief operations.*

The truth is, you can dedicate yourself to serving humanity no matter where you are in the world by being willing to respond to people in need both close by and far away. Whether you go far or stay close to home, you too can help people in need. You just have to be ready to go. Here are a few things you can do to be ready when you are called into action.

Love for People

One thing that distinguishes those who serve others is a genuine love for people. Whether you are simply being a good neighbor, volunteering locally, or going overseas, your professional ethics will include a pledge to help people without discrimination. For humanitarians, this pledge comes from the Red Cross principles, that we are to relieve suffering based on need alone. There is no question that every human being deserves help, regardless of nationality, race, religious beliefs, class or political opinions.

This imperative, this call to serve others in ways that look beyond individual identity, means seeing the one thing that matters most—*the human dignity in every person.* This means the people you are helping do not have to be a particular group; they do not have to be a certain age such as suffering children or distressed elderly, they do not have to look like you or share your racial identity, they do not have to share your religious beliefs or belong to a certain faith, their sexual preference does not matter, what they wear does not matter, their friends and their family and what neighborhood they live in or social status they belong to does not matter. The only thing that qualifies people to receive help is being human.

What does it mean, to love and care for people?

To love people is to genuinely care for their well-being. It means helping people who may, at times, seem unlovable. Serving others is not about reciprocity or what someone else can do for you. It is about taking the time to be present to another person and to see their need addressed.

Helping others without discrimination also means acting with compassion and seeing every person as deserving of basic needs and rights. It also means recognizing any bias, preference, or privilege you have based on your own identity and working to ensure that you are able to overcome those barriers to serve all people with integrity.

For example, when Hurricane Katrina hit New Orleans, the levees inundated streets and houses with water. Arriving upon the scene, a naked man ran up to me, asking where he could find clothes. He was in terrible shape, but I did not shy away from him. Everything he had was washed away. The only thing that mattered was that he needed help.

Here's another example of what it means to love people. When the young women I befriended in the slums of West Africa showed me their health cards revealing they were prostitutes, that did not change our friendship. They had to get monthly check-ups at the clinic to make sure they were not HIV positive. I was a student at the time. I wasn't running any major programs to change their lives. The only thing I could offer them was acceptance and solidarity. When they came back from the clinic, we sang and danced because they had "no diseases" that day.

You can love people by having empathy and compassion for those who are suffering.

Listen to what people have to say.
Be responsive to their specific needs.
Do not look away from someone with a special need.
Do not be afraid of the problem.
Be willing to address challenges head on.

You can do this by being on the lookout for vulnerable people who need your time and attention the most. Be attentive to them and know what to do when they present themselves. If you are unable to help, find someone who can. Be resourceful by referring people to other sources of help if needed.

Step Out of Your Comfort Zone

We already discussed the importance of stepping out of your comfort zone. Let's consider what this means in reality. While every charitable organization would like you to text a number to contribute funds to their cause, and you should consider donating (the mere price of a cup of coffee), to be a humanitarian you need to do more than send a text message. You have to go somewhere, often times to a place you do not know, where people don't share your culture or speak your language. You must go where the need is greatest. This means sacrificing your own comfort and adjusting your standard of living.

Being with people in need may make you feel uncomfortable, because you may come to realize that you are a well-off person. Recognizing that your race, nationality, education, and financial position puts you in a place where you are safe and your basic needs are met is something that can make you feel guilty when you encounter people who are constantly striving to make it through each day.

Managing these feelings is important because you cannot form genuine relationships motivated by guilt. Turn those feelings into something more productive like generosity, solidarity, and compassionate action. Be careful not to offer sympathy, because your role is to empower people. Playing into a victim-hero mentality which places you in a position of power over others is not the right perspective. Having a "savior complex" hurts your ability to develop relationships with people based on trust and mutual respect. While you may be privileged to help, you must also be ready to receive input and advice from a diverse team of people and the clients you are serving, both of whom will teach you important life lessons. Work with others in a spirit of humility and partnership, so that you can achieve results together as a team.

As a foreigner in another country, you will not be able to correct every wrong and make everything right. This phenomenon of bringing in answers from the outside is a trap, as explained in the book, *The White Man's Burden* by William Easterly. The book emphasizes that partnering with local people to identify local solutions is *the only sustainable path to development*. Easterly further outlines the harmful impact of foreign interventions that don't rely on local markets to spur growth. This perspective can be especially difficult for Americans who are used to a certain standard of living that is not easily replicated or even desirable in other contexts. It is critical, therefore, to ask people what they need the most and to work in partnership with local organizations to achieve results based on their own definition of success.

After many years of not recognizing the impact of foreign imports on the local economy, the humanitarian sector is trying to increase local procurement of supplies and food products to avoid flooding the market with cheap foreign products, which depresses local income and decreases revenue for local businesses. However, when food and critical supplies are not available in-country, they must be flown in from regional stockpiles that have been set up by aid agencies in logistics hubs strategically located around the world.

When you step out of your comfort zone and start to work in partnership with local communities, you still might find yourself tired and dirty at the end of the day. Water may be in short supply. There may not be enough water to take a shower. If there is a shower, it might only run cold water. You might only have a bucket and cup of water. There might not be any water at all, or worse yet, the water might be infected with bacteria that can make you sick.

Getting sick is a reality for people living in places with weak infrastructure and poor sanitation. This results in high health risks. Ensuring that you are healthy means getting immunizations, taking extra precaution with what you eat and drink, carrying emergency medical supplies with you when you travel, and anticipating your own medical needs wherever you go.

You may be hungry and thirsty. Following a major disaster, public markets tend not to function. Stores could be closed, collapsed, or looted. It will be hard for everyone to buy food and supplies. Until commerce is restored, it may be hard to sustain yourself let alone help others. Be prepared by bringing what you need and making sure that your organization is also prepared.

What would it mean for you to get out of your comfort zone? Here are a few examples of when I was really uncomfortable in the field.

While interviewing refugees in the slums of Manila, in the Philippines, one night I was awakened by tiny feet running all over my face—*mice. Mice!* I screamed, waking up the refugees sleeping on the floor next door. They laughed at me when they realized I was bothered by such a trivial thing—at least I had a bed to sleep on!

During the response to the Ebola epidemic in Sierra Leone, while testing protective clothing worn by doctors and nurses in rural health clinics, my team worked next to the maternity ward. All day long we could hear the screams of women giving birth without any pain medicine. We could almost feel their pain as the women shrieked for hours of painful labor, while we were learning how medical personnel prevented the Ebola virus from spreading. Amidst life and death, there was a mixture of constant screaming and prayers. Working under such conditions was not only hard, it was emotionally taxing.

When the team returned to our hotel at the end of the day, there was no air conditioning, the beds were dirty, and there was no running water. Flies were all over the food we had to eat for the night.

We had to ask ourselves, is it better to go hungry or to risk eating contaminated food? More importantly, who are we to ask for more in a time of Ebola?

When you get out of your comfort zone, remember that *your discomfort is minimal* compared to the suffering of people who are at-risk of losing their lives, their homes, and their livelihoods.

Manage your own discomfort by sharing your experience with colleagues. Celebrate the small victories each day. Those victories might include transporting a wounded person to a clinic, referring a child who is alone to a safe shelter, providing food to hungry people, and receiving refugees after a long journey. These are rewarding moments, even if achieving them can seem exhausting. If no one else is celebrating, make a celebration. Give an award. Recognize one another's hard efforts.

Take Risks

Helpers go where the need is greatest, where the beneficiaries are located. "Beneficiaries" are people who benefit from aid, often in the form of short-term projects that help people recover from critical events. This term is also changing as more organizations use the word clients to reflect a service-oriented approach.

Relief workers spend long days driving for hours to reach people who need help the most. These drives are not on smooth four-lane highways. They're on jostling roads that can be full of people, animals, and debris. Even if you have a strong stomach, you may get carsick from the rough journey.

You may be close to areas where there are landmines. These days, terrorist groups aren't just burying land mines in the ground. They're building small-scale improvised explosive devices (IEDs) that detonate under doorways, rocks in the street, and in toys to attract children. Your mine awareness can save your life and the lives of those around you. Before you go overseas, make sure your organization is making you aware of these and other location-specific security risks.

If you are going to a war zone, consider the threat to your personal safety as well as the threats facing beneficiaries in the area. Be well-informed. Research security incidents in the country and region where you are about to go, studying maps of violent incidents and understand the tactics of armed groups in the area. Reputable agencies will have security plans in place including incident response plans. Ask your agency for their plan before you go on mission. If they don't have one, reconsider whether to accept the position.

No matter how prepared your agency is, your physical safety is your personal responsibility. Cultivate good instincts. Calculate the risks you are taking in the field. Listen to yourself and those around you. Do not take unnecessary risks.

Your safety may also be compromised for reasons beyond your control and beyond the ability of your agency to respond. That is why many organizations prepare their staff with hostile environment training. Some agencies also require you to sign liability agreements stating that in the event of your death or injury, you will not hold the organization liable.

Some of the risks you will face can be calculated, others cannot, like driving in unsafe road conditions. I took great risk when I drove to work every day in South Africa, a country with relatively unregulated traffic laws.

I was nearly killed one morning when a drunk driver crashed into me in Johannesburg. At first, I felt lucky to be alive. But by the time I was taken to the hospital, I could not remember my name or address. I was in complete shock when they wheeled me into the emergency room. Male nurses speaking five different languages were trying to tell me that I might be paralyzed. They strapped me down to a table and tore off my clothes with large scissors. I was so far from home in that moment, I couldn't think of anyone to call. I wanted someone to be with me in that horrifying moment, but my mind was so blurry, I could not think straight. I eventually recovered with the help of good friends, but it was a hard time to be so far away from home.

Dangerous Journeys

You may also have to take dangerous journeys as part of your assignment. Depending on where you go, your gender can also make you vulnerable. When a donor for my project in Afghanistan suggested we expand to the north of the country, I took great risk to travel to the Iran border. The only partner organization I found to transport me there asked me to carry $50,000 in cash to their regional director. I was nervous to travel with a driver who didn't know me. He could have sold me to the highest bidder in the borderlands. Men also face certain vulnerabilities in the field, such as being susceptible to kidnapping, bribery and extortion, as well as forced recruitment into criminal or armed groups.

On the way up to the Iran border, we traveled over steep terrain during the winter months, putting chains on the tires so the truck would stick to ice coating the road. Each time we stopped to refuel, trucks of armed militia came beside us. I hid down in the back seat so no one could see that I was a woman. A foreign woman was a prime target for kidnapping.

I hoped the risk of traveling up to the border would be worth it. My goal was to assess conditions for displaced people to go home to those areas. My saving grace was meeting up with a team of Italian humanitarian workers who housed and fed me, providing me with a hot shower and local transport so I could accurately assess security conditions in the area. I learned that active fighting would soon lead to more displacement from this area. There was no way to safely expand operations closer to Iran. Had I not made the trip, I could have responded to the donor prematurely, placing staff and assets there and putting more people at even greater risk.

You might be asking: is the risk worth it? I hope my stories have shown you that when you go on mission, you are never alone. You are joining a group of talented people who are also sent there for the same purpose. Knowing your fellow humanitarians and coordinating with them can save your life and the lives of people around you. The comradery and friendships you form is one of the greatest rewards of being in the field.

Cultivate genuine friendships everywhere you go, and you will have the time of your life. I will never forget working in Afghanistan, when on Fridays (a Muslim holy day) colleagues gathered to play volleyball during the day and met in an underground bunker to dance at night.

One day, during the middle of a volleyball game, the International Committee of the Red Cross (ICRC) team stopped the game to receive a helicopter medical evacuation right there on site. Once they could assess the medical condition of the people being evacuated, they arranged for them to be received at a hospital in Pakistan. When the helicopter took off for Pakistan, they started the volleyball game up again, as if it was all in a day's work!

In the field, no man or woman is an island. When you are on mission, use all the resources available to you from within your team, in your organization, and from like-minded partners who have an interest in your shared success. Don't be afraid to ask for help and advice. And, whatever you do, don't become isolated from your team.

You can also manage risks by knowing the security conditions and operational policies before you go on an assignment. Ask for training on working in a hostile environment. Participate in security briefings. Heed warnings. Follow the rules set by security personnel. Take calculated risks and learn from each experience.

Above all else, make friends with people who believe in humanity like you do. Bring out the best in one other and spur one another on to do great things.

Live with Less

Another secret to success in the field, is learning how to live with less. When you get your first overseas assignment and are notified that your luggage must weigh less than 20 kilos (approximately 44 lbs.) to fit onto a humanitarian flight, you know that you have to pack light.

You may also need to pack another small "go" bag, with a few essentials in case you have to evacuate the area immediately. This includes packing personal identification documents, a change of clothes, and essential medicines. In some circumstances, you will need to be prepared to leave everything else behind at a moment's notice.

You will eventually come to realize that, not only do you have to *pack light*, you also have to *live light*. Do you really need all the things you've collected along life's way? In reality, human beings have few essential needs.

So, I learned to live light, and I never missed my things—the excess clothes and shoes—and other items. Each day I woke up and focused on the job at hand. If I needed anything that I didn't bring, I could eventually find it locally or within the region when I traveled for other supplies.

You, too, can live with less, not just if you go on a mission overseas. Right now, wherever you are, you can begin to weed out your excess things. Donate and sell items you do not need. Foregoing common luxuries, like going out to eat, can free up your budget to donate to a charitable cause.

If you want to donate items in a disaster or emergency response, the best method is to give cash. Donating used items and supplies can clog up airports and result in waste. Giving cash allows relief agencies to buy items locally, energizing the local markets. Some humanitarian agencies have also started giving out vouchers to refugees, allowing them to use virtual credit which enables them to customize their relief package. These developments are good for the sector and should be encouraged by donors.

Being willing to live with less also means relying on your ingenuity to get things done. Be resourceful by working collaboratively with your colleagues. To successfully help others, you will need to be creative and persuasive, encouraging yourself and others to go the extra mile to achieve results.

Humanitarians are skilled at observing a chaotic environment and assessing the situation to determine what is needed and who takes priority. Conducting a needs assessment is a fundamental task that every relief worker needs to know how to do. Doing an assessment is similar to the concept of medical triage when doctors and nurses must decide whom to save first. The assessment helps determine what is truly needed, to avoid duplication of effort and waste.

Even if you have a good amount of money to give away, you will not be able to help everyone. You must determine how many people you can help, what kind of help is needed most, where that help will go, to whom and for how long, and what the impact of the aid will be on that area. That is why humanitarian relief is a skilled, professional line of work, best done by people and organizations with experience working in difficult areas. Volunteers can make an extraordinary difference also when their skills are matched to the right agency.

When you cannot meet a need that you have identified, it's important not to wash your hands of the situation. Work with other agencies that may have the ability to meet the need.

For example, after Hurricane Matthew hit Haiti, my team identified that many children between the ages of 3 to 9 were vulnerable because they lost their parents. The schools were closed and being used as temporary shelters. Children were going without basic items such as clothes and shoes, causing them to go naked and wander in the streets.

Although my organization was not focused on child protection, we shared our assessment of the situation with every child-focused agency in the area to see how they could help. When the gap persisted, we sought special donations to provide the children with a distribution of clothes, shoes, and toys. We also partnered with a local organization that could follow up with the children and place them in caring families for their long-term recovery.

Personal Resilience

As a helper, you also need to grow in strength and courage to cultivate personal resilience. Often times, you will see and experience things that you cannot change. People will die and get hurt. Sick patients may never recover. Accidents will happen. These experiences will have an emotional impact on your life. You will need the personal strength to recover from what you have seen and be able to accept the things you could not do.

Personal resilience is about cultivating your ability to recover from shocks that are part of the job hazard. Having good mechanisms for self-care and the support of friends and family will be important to staying active in the humanitarian sector over the long-term. You will experience so many extreme things; you will need to share your stories with a close group of people who can listen and genuinely care about your experiences. Make the effort to stay in touch with people so they know what you are doing. Also, keep up your professional network so you can always reach out to fellow humanitarians in other organizations.

Sometimes resilience is about having the courage to right a wrong. I needed strength to approach another organization when I learned their food assistance program was only for HIV/AIDS patients, which gave hungry people an incentive to infect themselves with HIV in order to eat. I encouraged the organization to adopt a more holistic approach to address hunger in the area and prevent the spread of disease.

At other times, resilience is about acknowledging the root cause of a problem. For example, I needed to be resilient when I realized that the migrant children from Myanmar in our tsunami relief program were being abused every day. When they went home, they were vulnerable and unsafe. I had to expand our work from developing child-friendly spaces to changing harmful policies that denied migrant children the right to go to school in Thailand, where they would be better protected under adult supervision.

I also needed to be resilient when a plan I developed for evacuees after Hurricane Katrina was denied by the government because the focus of rebuilding New Orleans was on infrastructure, not people. I vowed to work against systemic racism and discrimination that left people to fend for themselves in the aftermath of the storm.

Ultimately, the life of a helper is full of rich rewards. When you take on a big problem, accepting a new job or going on a mission, you do not know what will happen. When you step into a challenging role or get on the plane to a new destination, you don't know who you will meet when you land. But you can be certain of a few things:

You will be surprised by joy. You will discover beautiful places and meet amazing people. You will make friends with people from many nations and with numerous belief systems. You will see the smiles of children and live in solidarity with those who are hurting.

The assistance you provide will be a welcome relief to many people. You will change lives by offering help when people need it most. The better world that you envision is being made possible every day, as you do the work to make things right. Some days will be better than others, but ultimately good will prevail.

When death, destruction, and violence try to overwhelm the good work you do, when you experience a dark night of the soul, you will need to step back and rest. You will have to rely on the strength of friends and colleagues to be renewed. You will see that your life is part of the lives of others—that you are only human, and that humanity has many gifts to give.

When you see that each person and place is capable of recovering and rebuilding, it is awesome to be part of transforming lives. Being with people in difficult circumstances, in times of crisis and disaster, provides you with a fresh perspective on the world. No matter how bad things get, good things are to come. Despite the losses you will experience, there is more to be gained. Amid death and destruction, you will meet people determined to rebuild their lives. You will see that time and time again, human resilience and determination arise, making everything possible.

If you love people and are willing to step out of your comfort zone, take risks, live with less, and cultivate personal resilience, then you have what it takes to serve a world in need. The world needs people like you. What will you do next?

1

YOU ARE NEEDED

*"A different world cannot be built
by indifferent people."*
Chinese Proverb

Journey to a Better World

I want to take you on a trip with me. It is the journey of a lifetime. We are going to places unknown, to help people we have not met but who are waiting for us. Pack your bags, grab your passport and your traveling shoes, and come along.

But, I also want to warn you. When we return, you may never be the same.

You could say that traveling is in my blood. The first time I flew overseas, I was in my mother's womb. I was born in a small, African village called Mumias in western Kenya where it hadn't rained for over a year. Everyone in the village was praying for rain to cover the fields so there would be food to harvest. Instead of rain, they received our small family of three that was about to be four people: one nurse, one teacher, my brother who was a toddler, and an infant about to be born. That was me, traveling overseas before I was even 1 day old.

Thus, I was born in a small, African village. When I came into the world, the village chief, elders, women, and medicine man prayed that I would be a good omen—that I would *Bring Rain*—a much needed form of relief in a year of drought. Even though they performed a rain dance to welcome me back from the hospital, the rains did not come. People went hungry due to a bad harvest.

Although I didn't bring the village what they wanted most—rain and relief—their hope for my life never let go of *me*. For the rest of my life, I wanted to bring relief to hungry and thirsty people. I wanted to answer their prayer that I would bring rain and relief to many people.

Little did I know it at the time, but making a difference in the world isn't as easy as it looks. After twenty years of working with refugees and people in crisis, I've learned that it's not about simply "doing good" or feeling good about yourself. Rather, helping people is about accepting the human condition and doing what you can where you can, maybe right down the street from you, or far away from home.

Helping others means taking risks and working to overcome the obstacles that hold people back. In order to make an impact on people's lives, you have to be willing to take a look at your own life and be willing to change yourself.

Here's how I learned what really makes a difference—and a few other lessons along the way. I wrote this book to help bridge the gap between wanting to help others and realizing what it takes to get it done. This book will help you to be prepared for your unique purpose and mission in life so you can survive and thrive in a chaotic world.

When you venture out into the unknown, anything is possible. Before you put yourself out there, I want you to be as prepared as possible.

It's hard to say whether I chose to be a humanitarian relief worker or whether this path chose me. I have been attuned to the needs of people in crisis since the day I was born. Over the past twenty years, I have worked to help humanity from Maine to Washington, from Africa to Asia, the Middle East to the Caribbean. I've learned a few things along the way that I want to share with you as you consider your life purpose.

My own life has taken a number of twists and turns, and yours will too. When I was in my twenties, I wanted to diversify my work assignments as much as possible to ensure that I had experience in different regions and was seen as a global expert in refugee crises. As I entered my thirties, I tried to address the root causes of violence and instability that I saw on assignments. This meant working with governments and donors to increase funding for conflict prevention and humanitarian crises and to change restrictive policies that denied refugees their rights. In my forties, I focused on the physical safety of people who live in constant fear of armed conflict by training military, police, and peacekeepers on providing security for vulnerable populations.

All of these efforts brought me to where I am today—with a firm belief that the world needs more helpers—people just like you and me—who want to make a difference. **The question is, how should we go about the business of helping?**

Being a Helper

At what point in life do you find yourself? Stop and consider all the ways you have helped others. What core beliefs and ideas have motivated you? Whether you are involved in community service as a volunteer or donor, or you work on international projects as a professional career, you can make a difference in so many ways. This book will help you discover your unique path as you seek to do more.

All around us, people are in need. Locally, regionally, and around the world. What makes us stop and pay attention to the people who are hurting right around us? Given all the demands on our time and money, it takes real effort to focus our energy. Yet, the world needs people like you and me who care about others. The world needs passionate people who are willing to go from the sidelines to the frontlines in order to make a difference. There is an exciting road ahead on this journey. It begins with you.

On this journey, we will go to far-off places and also stay close to home. You might get closer to your own community in a more meaningful way than ever before. You will make the friends of a lifetime, doing great things. Even in the scary places, you will see that the world is ultimately a good place. The awareness you develop from getting to know new places and people will sharpen your view of things, and you will be changed.

The truth is, you don't need to go very far to make a difference. The chance to help and make a difference is vast. The opportunities are everywhere. You just need to see the world with new eyes and be ready to act when the time comes.

You may be wondering, what is wrong with the world? The constant cycle of bad news can wear you down. You may already have more responsibility than you can handle, caring for the needs of your own family. But you wish you could do more.

You may be a student, wondering what your life will be like after your studies. You are already involved in your community, but you feel there has to be more out there. *What else can you do?*

You may be deep into your career, but it's not as fulfilling as you thought it would be. Working for a paycheck and material things just doesn't seem like enough. *What more is out there for you?*

You may be close to retirement from your career, still feeling energetic, wanting a fresh vision, and looking for new ways to contribute. You have been to lots of places. You have experience, but you don't know how to share that experience with others. *What do you have that is needed the most?*

Perhaps you're a spiritual person, someone with faith, and you believe that helping others is an important part of expressing that faith. But you may wonder, *What kind of help is most meaningful?*

No matter what stage of life you are in, there is more you can do and be. If you feel the pull to help people, you are being called to a greater purpose. There is more waiting for you—more ways to contribute than you can imagine and more meaningful ways to engage with the world around you. Could a life of service be for you?

You might be asking yourself: **What can I do?** It's a good thing to consider your options up front. There is no shortage of problems you can work to address, from reducing the impact of climate change to ending gun violence and achieving racial equality, everywhere you turn there is something to do. What path will you choose?

People in your life may expect you to become a doctor—or perhaps a banker—to make a certain amount of money for your family or lifestyle. How will these expectations affect your choices? ***Are you ready to forge your own unique path?***

Going Beyond

If you want to go on this journey of a lifetime, to help people beyond borders, whether you are volunteering for a service project or embarking on an international career, you need to be prepared. Taking this path may require moving to a new place, adjusting your salary expectations, simplifying your way of life, redefining your basic needs, and reworking your definition of success. Remember, doing cross-cultural work does not always mean going overseas. You can start right where you are, from home.

Having success in changing lives is about more than good intentions. In addition to being willing, you also have to learn how to find real solutions to big problems by listening to people so you can understand what is actually needed.

Some of the problems you encounter, such as the root causes of poverty and violence, will be bigger than what you can achieve as one person. You may also have to reconcile with harsh social, political, and economic realities about why people suffer and have patience when you realize how long it is going to take to fundamentally change conditions in our society.

No matter what path you chose, the reward of helping others will far outweigh the costs. You will make friends with diverse groups of people from all over the world and learn to speak new languages (and how to get by on charades when necessary). You will find that people have a universal language, and that language is one of caring and compassion.

You will see lives changed and be grateful to be part of this transformation. You will also experience deep gratitude for the way people touch your life and change you as a person. When you make new friends who share your mission, you will feel deeply fulfilled by working together for a common cause.

Yes, I can tell you for sure—

the good life is one that is lived in service to others,

whether it's to those near you or to people far away.

Maybe you're wondering if you really have it in you. You might be apprehensive about the challenges you will encounter stepping out of your comfort zone and into a new neighborhood. You know it won't be easy to leave the comforts of home, whether you're helping across the street or around the world.

You want to say "yes" to the journey because you want to see the world. You want to experience all that life has to offer. When you step out into the unknown, you will find new friends and create unforgettable memories. By being a part of a community and surrounding yourself with good people, you will surmount every challenge that comes across your path.

When you set off to change the world, you will find that you are the one who will be changed. Let me share with you from my experience why I know you can do this.

Starting Out

When I set out to help people in crisis, I knew that each assignment would take a great amount of determination and sacrifice. I had no idea, really, that it would also take personal strength and courage to overcome difficult circumstances, that I was entering a world that was unpredictable, and that I would have to adapt to new ways of seeing things.

When I was in college, I used to wonder; *What will my life be like?* I always wanted my life to be *anything but ordinary*. I got my wish.

Answering the call to serve humanity has been extraordinary. Now that you know how much helping others can shape your life, I want to tell you how things worked out for me. From my decades of experience, I want to give you the tools to help you figure out how to live a rewarding life.

As you will discover in this book, there were times when I was held hostage and chased by crowds of angry men. I nearly died in a terrible car crash and again from a poisonous spider bite. I lost a good friend, and I gained so many more. Humanitarian work has given me a lifetime of friends and extraordinary experiences. I wouldn't trade it for anything.

Contrary to popular belief, you do not need to be a "super-hero" or a "saint" to save lives. You do not need to commit to a lifestyle of poverty to help others. You do not need to renounce all possessions like Mother Teresa did or be a paci-fist like Gandhi. You can be your ordinary self and choose to do extraordinary things. Consider the life of Samantha Smith, who at only 10 years old wrote a letter to the President of Russia telling him she did not want a nuclear war. Smith, who hails from my home state of Maine, became a young emissary visiting Russian leaders, encouraging them to make peace with the United States. Or, consider the life of Lual Mayen from Sudan, who grew up in a refugee camp much like the ones I am about to describe to you in this book, who is now design-ing video games that teach people how to "stay alive" in a war zone, how to help refugees like him, and what it takes to put countries on a path to peace.

In response to the call to help, I became an aid worker. Today, answering your call could mean taking an entirely dif-ferent approach. Yes, the world needs more aid workers to go out into the field. Every crisis could use more money and people to meet needs on the ground.

Yet, we could also use a better way of life, a better way of caring for people, to take hold among all nations. We could use a common belief in the worth and dignity of all people regardless of gender, race, religion, nationality, political opinion, sexual preference, or social group. We need more people who care for nature and the environment that sustains life. We need a better way of living that brings us more joy. Your specific and personal mission can help bring about that way of living.

You can "be" and "do" many things to contribute to a better world. You could become a climate scientist and prevent natural disasters by mitigating the risk of extreme weather patterns.

The world needs environmentalists to plant trees and clean up waste, and advocates for environmental protections so that people can live healthier, more sustainable lives.

You could invent new technologies so people who speak different languages can communicate better across geographic boundaries.

The world needs people who understand big data to study patterns of violence in order to make the outbreak of conflict more predictable and improve early warning.

Facts matter—however inconvenient they may be. You could work in social media and journalism, bearing witness by clearly speaking the truth.

You could be a doctor, public health specialist, or epidemiologist tracking the outbreak of epidemics and curing diseases.

You can also be a student, a parent, and a concerned citizen who uses your voice to uplift others within your community.

You can also be an accountant, artist, business owner, engineer, lawyer, teacher, or social worker and be involved in service projects in numerous ways.

Helpers are ordinary people who do extraordinary things. They are ready to act when the need arises, wherever they happen to be in the world.

The world needs more leaders who care about people and are accountable for their actions. You could run for office and be a political leader who looks out for the needs of others. Your diplomatic work can help bring an end to conflict. You can help create conditions for peace and prosperity.

The humanitarian sector also needs people in business and finance to overcome gaps in funding and to offer refugees jobs instead of handouts so they can live a dignified life, becoming self-reliant and meeting their own needs.

The world needs more people to make their way from the sidelines of life to center stage. It needs more people participating in the political process and the global economy. It needs people who are dedicated to social progress that are equally committed to pursuing justice and equality.

The world needs you.

Kenya

My journey started in the summer of 1992 when I was 15 years old. I raised enough money to help build a school in western Kenya, in a town called Kisumu. Every day our team of volunteers would get up and load trucks with construction supplies to build the school. We were digging trenches in thick, red clay to lay the foundation of the building when one morning, we were unable to access the land.

Overnight, hundreds of refugees from Somalia had gathered there, squatting on the seemingly open and available space. Kenyan police and United Nations vehicles descended upon the scene, quickly trying to figure out what to do with all the people.

I was just a teenager, and I was shocked as I stood there, watching the scene unfold. I was full of questions, with no easy answers.

In that moment, I wanted to do more for the refugees. I wanted to know everything about what can be done to help people fleeing war and violence. Of this I was convinced: *they deserved a better life.*

Now, more police cars were arriving on the scene, shouting angry-sounding words at the crowd of unhappy people. I realized that even in a country as hospitable as Kenya, they were unwelcome guests.

I looked at the faces of the Somali refugees before us. As the Kenyan police shouted at them, the women and children sat down on the ground, looking exhausted and weak. Their shoulders sagged; their faces looked gaunt. Their clothes were dusty. They had to be hungry and thirsty. One woman right in front of me was trying to nurse her baby, nudging the child gently, but it seemed too listless to want nourishment.

They must have traveled a long way, I thought. *How bad does it have to be in your home country for you to risk your life escaping with nothing but the clothes on your back?*

As our group stood there, picks and shovels in hand, the pastor and our group leader conferred about what to do next. In a few moments, they came up to us, a team of wide-eyed young people witnessing a mix of human misery and confusion.

"There's nothing much you can do here today," the pastor shrugged.

"Go see if the teachers need help in their classrooms," our leader suggested.

The teachers were glad to have us. As for me, I couldn't focus on the happy Kenyan children before me, all of them dressed in clean clothes and smiling, eager to learn. My eyes were drawn to the windows, peering out to see what would happen next. The children did not notice what was happening outside. We were singing songs about the love of Jesus when I saw numerous, large dump trucks arrive. My heart sank.

The police began using their fists and night sticks to beat the refugees onto the dump trucks. What kind of tent city were they hauling these refugees to? Or, after their harrowing escape, were they just being taken back to the border and dropped back into the dreadful situation from which they had fled?

Outside the classroom window, dust from the arriving dump trucks had turned the air into a choking cloud. I could hear coughing and women crying.

How can you not offer simple, human consideration to people just because they are a different nationality, I wondered?

Although you could say that Kenyan and Somali people looked alike because they are both African, they have a very different ethnic and linguistic makeup—something that I didn't really understand at the time. The Kenyan people did not want foreigners coming into their towns and villages, squatting on their land and forcing their way into the society and culture. They wanted to preserve their way of life.

But at what cost to other human beings?

That's why the dump trucks kept coming. Huge, filthy vehicles intended to take out the trash were sent to clean up the land where Somali refugees spent the night. That place just happened to be the land we purchased with donations for the school—but we didn't have any say in what happened next.

As I kept watching, my eyes following the situation while my lips sang songs with the school children, I saw other vehicles coming into the area. Large, white all-terrain vehicles with United Nations logos appeared. Men and women in blue vests with the insignia for the UN High Commissioner for Refugees stepped out of the cars to investigate.

The women's crying had turned into wailing. The men were resisting being shoved into the dump trucks. Even through the cinderblock walls of the classroom, I could feel the tension outside.

The UN monitors walked around and talked to people—but when the police started used riot batons and fists to beat the women and children into the trucks, they did not stop them.

What are you doing? I wanted to scream out the window. *Stop it!* I yelled from within. These are human beings—men, women, and children. No one should be treated that way.

By the end of the day, all the refugees had been rounded up and taken away. *To where? To what uncertain future and fate? How did those people feel—with their lives and the lives of their children and elderly hanging in the balance?*

Where does the impulse to help others come from? For me, it was bearing witness to the suffering of innocent people that shook me out of my complacency. I sensed their tremendous need, pain, fear, and confusion all at once. It came from wondering how the police could beat women and children, force them onto dirty dump trucks, and haul them away like they were trash to be disposed of. How could the United Nations representatives stand there, just observing the situation? Couldn't they do something more for these desperate people?

The day after the refugees were hauled away, we continued digging the foundation for the school. But I kept looking for more information about what happened to them. I picked up local papers showing pictures of refugees being hauled away all over the country. The news stories said the Somali refugees would be taken to Dadaab camp to the north near the Somali border and that other refugees from Sudan would be taken to a camp called Kakuma in the west.

When the summer drew to a close and it was time to leave Kenya, I packed up a collection of newspaper articles about the refugees so that I could remember them. As our team said their goodbyes at the airport in Nairobi, each of us going home to our school and our parents, I had the nagging feeling that there was something more to be done. But what and how?

That was the first of many refugee populations I would encounter in the years ahead. Since the early 1990s, refugee crises have grown tremendously—from 20 million refugees in 1992—to 80 million people displaced from their home in 2020. This unprecedented growth in the number of people leaving home is due to ongoing conflict in several countries, including Syria, Afghanistan, South Sudan, Myanmar, and Venezuela. While competition for power and resources continues in these contexts, countless numbers of civilians are forced to flee home to save their lives. As I helped provide relief to people in need, I began to wonder: was it also possible to keep them safe from harm in the first place?

2

Understanding Root Causes

"The complexities of almost every international crisis mean that even a generally positive outcome is messy and involves tradeoffs that do not resolve the issues at the root of conflict."

Samantha Power, *The Education of an Idealist*
Former U.S. Ambassador to the United Nations

That first refugee situation I encountered in Kenya felt a bit overwhelming. In fact, sad to say, it was hardly a blip on the screen of a global refugee crisis that would erupt in the coming years. When it comes to helping people, I have learned that you have to do more than provide immediate relief. You have to also understand the root cause of the problem.

What is behind all the chaos in the world?

Chronic Instability

Today, wars tend to last ten years or longer. Nearly 2.5 million people have died as a result of armed conflict in the last decade.[2] Natural disasters are becoming more frequent because of climate change. Therefore, as an aid worker, you may find

---

[2]Pettersson, Therese and Oberg, Magnus. Uppsala Conflict Data Program (UCDP), Trends in Organized Violence, 1989-2019, Journal of Peace Research, June 2020.

yourself working in countries that are experiencing chronic instability and recurring crises. It's important to understand the root causes of the problems you're working to address. War and poverty are two main drivers of displacement, resulting from poor governance and inequitable economic growth.

Over time, my journey to a career in humanitarian work started by getting involved in volunteer service, then getting a good education. Once I finished my studies, I gained experience by going overseas to assist refugees, then I became an advocate for policy changes to improve the way governments manage crises. Eventually, I started working with the military to improve the physical security of people in conflict zones. Each assignment from Kenya to the Philippines, Afghanistan to Haiti, exposed me to new dimensions of emergency response. Moreover, what I witnessed on assignment compelled me to address the root causes of the problems that create humanitarian crises in the first place.

That same refugee camp in Kenya where the Somali people were off-loaded from dump trucks still holds over 220,000 people, some of whom have lived there **for the last 20 years.** It is the third largest refugee camp in the world. The largest refugee camp is Kutupolong camp in Bangladesh, which holds over 600,000 people. A Muslim minority from Myanmar called the Rohingya have lived there since 2017, after escaping ethnic cleansing by the military.

Another large camp, Bidi Bidi in Uganda, houses over 250,000 refugees from neighboring South Sudan who are scared to go home due to conflict between different ethnic groups and political parties. These large camps represent thousands of lives on hold, people waiting for conditions to change in their home countries so they can return home. Due to ongoing conflict, some of them will never return to where they came from.

At the time I am writing this, the United Nations reports that nearly 80 million people are uprooted from their homes, with over 26 million people living as refugees outside their country of origin, 45 million who are living as internally displaced persons (IDPs) within their country, and another 4 million migrants who are waiting for their asylum claims to be processed.[3] According to the United Nations, most of these refugees come from five countries: Afghanistan, Myanmar, South Sudan, Syria, and Venezuela. Each of these countries struggles to have a representative government that can administer services, mediate disputes between different factions, and foster conditions for economic growth.

Let's consider how the people who humanitarian agencies seek to help are often stuck in situations far beyond their control.

What it Means to be "Stuck"

To help you understand how humanitarian problems are entrenched in broader economic, social, and political problems, let me give you some examples of what it means to be stuck in circumstances beyond your control.

When I first arrived in Haiti, I heard that the earthquake had crumbled most government buildings downtown in the area known as Champ de Mars. One particular building was of special concern to me, the National Archives which held identity documents of every person born in Haiti, including birth certificates and passports.

---

[3]United Nations High Commissioner for Refugees (UNHCR), Refugee Figures at a glance, 18 June 2020.

As I approached the destroyed building, I saw groups of men burning tattered documents representing the lives of countless individuals in large trash barrels, generating heat to cook by the fire. There would be nothing left of the archive to preserve—the nation's entire history was in danger of being lost.

Although I went to determine what was left of the building, my attention was soon drawn to one person, an elderly woman sitting nearby. She was not looking for documents, she was not burning them or trying to cook. She sat there, on a huge pile of paper, with her hands cusped around her chin and a blank look on her face, staring out into nothing.

The hard look on her face was one of disbelief mixed with grief. From the deep lines of wrinkles in her face down to the thin frame of her body, I guessed she was about 80 years old.

By this time, she had lived through five military coups and under seven other administrations, all offering people freedoms that come from a democratically elected government. She had also lived through numerous flash floods, hurricanes, and other political storms that raised food prices and made the country dependent on aid.

I looked at her for a long time—she did not move. There was no one around her, which was strange as people congregated closer to one another than ever before in the days after the quake. It looked like she had no one to cling to and no energy left to survive another disaster.

How Humanitarian Aid Works

In a large-scale emergency response, different humanitarian agencies divide up responsibility for a specific location or refugee camp based on who can respond to specific needs. There are United Nations agencies and nongovernmental organizations (NGOs) that specialize in providing food aid, shelter, water and sanitation, medical care, and other types of support to displaced populations. These specialties are organized by what the United Nations calls "clusters" or sectors of response.

There are numerous sectors of humanitarian response in total including food, nutrition, shelter, water and sanitation (WASH), camp management, health, logistics, protection, telecommunications, and early recovery, with emerging sectors such as the environment and land rights. Each sector is led by a United Nations agency in cooperation with NGOs. For example, there is a logistics cluster that organizes the shipments of aid from various ports and airport runways. The logistics cluster is led by the United Nations World Food Program (WFP), which won the Nobel Peace Prize for its life-saving work getting food to people in conflict zones.

WFP also stockpiles critical supplies in regional hubs around the world. These warehouses contain the anticipated needs of countries that are vulnerable to disaster so that aid can be shipped out quickly when needed. The WFP needs transport and heavy lift capabilities to deliver food aid and readily offers its warehouses as storage for other response sectors and international agencies.

Humanitarian agencies with similar goals organize meetings by sector so they can coordinate and ensure the population's needs are covered. These clusters work to reduce duplication of effort and increase aid effectiveness. They also liaise with local government officials and affected communities under the umbrella organization, the United Nations Office for the Coordination of Humanitarian Affairs (OCHA).

Aid agencies assist people affected by crises by providing for their basic needs. However, assistance is only part of what is needed. People also need protection, safety from harm, and a recognition of their basic human rights.

The UN Protection Cluster has a mandate to work alongside governments and other authorities to ensure that affected people, including refugees and displaced populations, have the recognition they need to live with dignity. The protection cluster is led by the United Nations High Commissioner for Refugees (UNHCR) with support from other agencies specializing in child protection, gender-based violence, and human rights.[4] Protection agencies negotiate legal and policy issues which impact people's lives, such as where they can live and whether they can work or go to school. Sometimes they intervene in individual circumstances, but oftentimes they are looking out for the needs of groups of people that are particularly vulnerable.

For example, while managing a large UN protection project for displaced people in Afghanistan, I frequently went to the governor of the Province of Kandahar for permission to do certain things. I was not the only aid worker who did this—the UN had to negotiate Memoranda of Understanding (MoU) with the governor's office to establish camps for displaced people, which included the right to use the land for a certain period of time.

One day, I went to the governor to appeal for Fatima, a woman who had lost her husband and both of her sons in the conflict. She wanted to travel to the capital city of Kabul, but

---

[4]The UN Protection Cluster is comprised of numerous agencies with distinct specialties including the International Organization for Migration (IOM), UN High Commissioner for Human Rights (OHCHR), UN Children's Agency (UNICEF), UN Mine Action, and nongovernmental organizations that protect refugees and displaced persons in emergencies.

police at checkpoints kept taking her out of the buses going north. She did not have a travel pass to proceed further, and she was not traveling with a male relative. Fatima was not yet old enough to go unnoticed by the young soldiers. They thought she was being improper by traveling alone.

I asked the governor to grant Fatima a special pass with his signature that would allow her to travel to the capital. When I appealed to the governor, the men surrounding him laughed.

"What good is this woman on her own? She is no use to anyone," they smirked.

"That's right," I said. *"What use is she to you? Let her go and be with her family."*

I handed the governor a letter that I drafted, offering his blessing for her travel. The letter also named her male relatives awaiting her arrival in Kabul. The governor signed it with his seal, and Fatima was on her way.

Refugee Self-Reliance

In the situation I described earlier in Kenya, there were hundreds of thousands of refugees whose needs had to be considered as a group. The government decided that refugees from neighboring countries like Somalia should be placed in camps. At the onset of an emergency, UNHCR negotiates a Memorandum of Understanding about where camps are to be located and how they should be managed.

This policy of encampment, however, discouraged people from settling locally, thus preventing them from integrating into the population. Placing refugees in camps and restricting their freedom of movement makes it difficult for them to find work and become self-reliant. For a long time, refugees in Kenya were subject to the goodwill of foreign aid, which created dependency and a sense of hopelessness for those who were unable to resettle in other countries.

It takes more than giving aid to make a difference in the lives of refugees. It also takes advocating for policy changes to make it legal for refugees to live and work among the local population. If refugees are allowed to work and earn a living, they are less dependent on foreign aid. While living on food rations may be necessary at the onset of an emergency, which can endure for months, as conflicts drag on for years, standing in line for handouts and food rations is no way to live. Also, refugees cannot sustain enough nutritional requirements on emergency supplements alone. They need a varied diet of meats, vegetables, grains, and dairy just like you and me. They need to purchase a range of food items and other products with money they earned through working.

Also, refugee children are often restricted from getting a formal education. If a refugee child can go to school, then that child has hope for the future. When left alone in a camp with nothing to do, children are often abused and exploited. Boys can be taken by armed groups and forcibly recruited as soldiers. Young girls are forced into early marriage so they have another adult to provide for them. This is no way for a child to grow up.

Abraham's Story

Consider the story of Abraham Awolich, a refugee from Sudan who lived in Kakuma Camp in Kenya from the age of 12 until he was 22 years old:

"I left Sudan because of the war. Everyone was a target. The only option was to leave the country hoping

to go to a safer place.... As I and others fled, there was danger everywhere...we lacked water, food, protection, and transportation. I became sick from drinking dirty water. We ate wild leaves and fruits that caused stomach problems.

The camp was a little safer than Sudan because there was no aerial bombardment. We also could not work or travel outside the camp. So literally it was an open-air prison, a storage place for human beings.

The good thing in the camp was the school...from kindergarten to the 12ᵗʰ grade. Even if you were lucky to go to school, it was a dead end. You couldn't go any further. My dream was to become someone important in my community...to get a PhD or start a business or work in the government.... But I lost hope, fearing I may end there forever."[5]

Abraham's story is shared by countless other refugees who flee a country only to find that harsh political realities in exile make it difficult for them to move forward with their lives. Thankfully, Abraham was eventually resettled in the United States where he could begin to work toward his dream.

Abraham was resettled by the U.S. Committee for Refugees and Immigrants (USCRI). I worked for USCRI for many years, coordinating a global network of organizations that advocated for policy changes to allow refugees the right to work, go to school, and access local services such as health care. These basic human rights were recognized in the 1951 UN Refugee Convention, but governments became dependent on foreign

---

[5]Refugee Voices, Ten Years in Kenya: an Interview with Abraham Awolich, *Refugee Reports*, May 2004.

aid to address the problem. Instead of integrating refugees into the local population, host countries put refugees in camps where their suffering was visible to the media, drawing more international aid.

The leadership of USCRI put pressure on governments to grant refugees greater freedom of movement outside of camps.[6] This advocacy resulted in a UN policy on Alternatives to Camps, promoting the idea of refugee self-reliance.[7] In 2019, the UN further developed a Global Compact on Refugees with governments signing onto commitments to expand refugee access to work and educational opportunities.[8] A big part of these commitments was recognizing that with the increasing number of displaced people in the world, it would not be possible to keep them all in camps to provide for their needs.

New Models of Aid

Today, with the support of the World Bank and the UN Refugee Agency, Kenya has embarked on an innovative pilot project, the Kalobeyei settlement that allows refugees to work and pursue economic development alongside local communities. The settlement is providing 20,000 refugees with an opportunity to live with freedom and dignity by allowing them to live and move among the local population, go to work, and go to school. The project is a win-win solution that was not possible ten years

---

[6]USCRI launched the anti-warehousing campaign after releasing the World Refugee Survey in 2004.

[7]For more information, see the UNHCR Policy on Alternatives to Encampment, July 2014.

[8]The UN Global Compact for Refugees and Migrants was signed by 164 countries in December 2018.

ago. The project is also improving basic services and infra-structure for Kenyan people who live alongside refugees. It was made possible by numerous people in government and financial institutions who worked alongside humanitarians to reconsider lasting solutions to refugee problems. It used to be that refugees had only three options for durable solutions to their plight:

1. Return home
2. Local integration
3. Resettlement to a third country

Now, governments and financial institutions are working on creative solutions that provide uprooted people with more dignified ways to live in exile. These alternative pathways include legal migration, educational scholarships, and temporary employment—all of these options offer refugees hope for their future while they wait for a permanent solution.

Changing the way refugees are assisted became even more important after a million Syrian refugees moved to Europe in 2015. These refugees had lived in camps throughout the Middle East for five years. Seeing that the war in Syria was far from over, refugees decided to move on and seek a new life. This movement overwhelmed European states where refugees sought asylum, and the European Union tried to stem the flow of people coming through Turkey.

As you can see, being a humanitarian is about far more than providing a Band-Aid or a bed for the night, as some people have suggested.[9] It is about identifying ways to reduce

---

[9]David Rieff, journalist and author of *A Bed for the Night: Humanitarianism in Crisis* (2014), claims that the neutrality of humanitarian agencies was compromised by donor governments who did not address the root causes of genocide in Rwanda and ethnic cleansing in Bosnia, which required swift political action to save lives.

the vulnerability of people in crisis and adopting innovative approaches that produce lasting results.

Applying humanitarian aid strategically can foster conditions that result in greater stability. For example, a quick response to a disaster that saves lives makes it easier to preserve the human capital necessary to rebuild critical infrastructure. After Hurricane Katrina hit New Orleans, the State of Louisiana wanted to keep as many people close to the city as possible so that they could begin spending money and rebuilding homes.

However, there are things that short-term relief cannot achieve. Humanitarian aid is not a substitute for political action, which is needed in places like Yemen, where Saudi Arabia has been conducting a proxy war with Iran. Nor can humanitarian aid create the security conditions to prevent large-scale violence in South Sudan, where ethnic divisions have undermined national unity. Short-term aid alone does not have the power to end poverty in places like Haiti, where people live on $2 a day despite billions of dollars of aid pouring into the country over the years.

Yet, **aid saves lives and reduces the suffering of people in need.** When countries come together through decision-making bodies like the United Nations, they put pressure on governments to provide aid for their people. Negotiating humanitarian access in conflict zones includes working toward pauses in fighting through ceasefire agreements and opening up transportation routes and commercial ports that are necessary to get the economy functioning again. This process of high-level negotiations is also known as "humanitarian diplomacy," which has been critical to getting supplies to people inside war-torn Syria, for example.

When a conflict like the war in Syria wages on for years, donors start looking for ways to transition aid from short-term relief to long-term development. Making this relief to development transition is especially difficult when it is not possible to negotiate financial agreements with a federal government. Multilateral financial agencies like the World Bank and International Monetary Fund (IMF) provide funding to governments, which allows them to strengthen institutions that serve the people. For example, this might include financing a central bank that allows civil servants to be paid a salary so they do not depend on bribes and turn to corruption to make a living.

If the central government is persecuting its people and causing violence, donors are more interested in supporting a peace process that will stop the fighting than building institutions that offer services to people. Yet, in order for refugees to return home to rebuild their lives, they need some measure of confidence that basic support systems, like finance and telecommunications services, health and educational facilities, and water and sanitation systems are functioning.

Capacity Building

In countries with functional governments, we tend to take these basic services for granted. Yet when a country is lacking basic infrastructure and services, these systems can get co-opted by terrorist groups and criminal gangs who exert control over essential supplies to control the population. This is how armed groups like Al-Shabaab have retained control over Somalia, using illegal taxation and control of humanitarian supply routes to finance violence against the federal government.

In countries experiencing chronic instability, such as Haiti, it's common for humanitarian response agencies to work alongside long-term development agencies, like the World Bank, and financial institutions that work on structural reforms to the central government. It's also common to work alongside weak government institutions that have a difficult time providing services to the population. Humanitarian aid is not a substitute for good governance, but if done right, including local government officials in the response, it can support the transition from short-term assistance to long-term recovery.

After the earthquake struck Haiti, it was important to involve local government officials in humanitarian cluster meetings and to organize humanitarian coordination efforts within municipal offices. This helped get local government officials up and running, addressing people's needs neighborhood by neighborhood.

In Afghanistan, government agencies that existed on a federal organization chart may have been nothing more than three people sitting around a desk with no pen, papers or computers to help them function. This lack of administration and infrastructure creates a cycle of dependency on international assistance in many countries with recurring instability. Humanitarian agencies often compensated for local officials who did not have vehicles or gasoline by including them in site visits to affected communities and, in some cases, by reimbursing them for related travel costs.

While humanitarian relief would ideally have a time limit—of, say, three years—so that long-term development agencies can focus on achieving stability in partnership with local governments, relief is often needed on a recurring basis. This is because weak governments do not have the institutions necessary to provide basic services to their people. Lack of good governance can undermine humanitarian efforts, but aid can also work to strengthen and build the capacity of legitimate government institutions. By working alongside national counterparts who can support aid prioritization and delivery, you can foster a deeper understanding of how aid works and hold governments accountable to meeting the needs of their people.

War Zones

War disrupts normal life. It forces people to make difficult choices, such as whether to stay in their homes when they fear aerial bombardment or to leave their homes and become refugees in countries where they have an unknown future. To reduce the threats that civilians face during war, armed groups need to respect the fundamental principles of international law.

Improving the conduct of war to make it less costly to civilian lives is a major undertaking. The Geneva Conventions, which make up the Law of Armed Conflict (LOAC), make it clear that civilians who are not directly participating in hostilities and have not joined an armed group are not a legitimate military target and are to be respected by all parties to the conflict. This means that every combatant who is fighting should follow the law.

Today, many non-state armed groups and terrorist organizations use civilians as human shields to avoid being attacked by traditional military forces governed by the laws of armed conflict. Nonetheless, international law prohibits inhumane and degrading treatment of prisoners of war and of the civilian population. These assurances are found in Common Article 3 of the Geneva Conventions. Fundamental guarantees apply whether state armies are fighting a formally declared international armed conflict between two countries or whether non-state actors are engaged in terrorism and other forms of non-international armed conflict.

This might sound complicated, but it's really important because if you are working in a conflict zone, you will need to understand which armed groups are operating in the area and how they function. If you want to protect yourself and others from violence, you will need to find ways to hold government authorities and armed actors accountable for their actions. This is especially true in latent conflicts where all sides are inflicting suffering on the population.

For example, parts of Ukraine have been occupied by Russian forces since 2014. In the Eastern Territories, the region is divided by a contact line spanning 500 kilometers. Since the invasion, the Ukrainian government has been unable to administer financial and social services like banking and pensions that older people rely on for financial support.

Thus, if a Ukrainian citizen wants to use a national bank, he has to cross the contact line. Thousands of people cross the contact line every day, waiting for hours to go through dangerous checkpoints.[10] International monitors with the Organization for Security and Co-operation in Europe (OSCE) observe these movements to make sure people's rights are protected by authorities on both sides.

---

[10]Stern, David L. "These Ukrainians have a pension awaiting. But they literally have to cross a minefield to get it." *The Washington Post,* January 13, 2019.

Meanwhile in communities to the East, while male relatives cross the contact line, oftentimes women and children are left at home where armed forces are occupying their neighborhood. Some military units have taken over fortified buildings including schools, which is contrary to international law. While young men are out of school, they are recruited into "youth groups" by Russian forces trying to win over the population. Imagine that while a man crosses the contact line to cash a check from his bank, he worries whether his family will still be there when he returns home at the end of the day.

This is why humanitarian protection agencies like the UN Children's Fund (UNICEF) establish safe places for children in conflict zones to keep them away from armed groups and why other organizations offer ways for women to earn a living. Other specialized agencies like the International Committee of the Red Cross (ICRC), are working with militaries on both sides of the conflict, reminding them that occupying schools and recruiting young men into the armed forces is contrary to international law. Humanitarians work to help government officials and military forces take corrective action that allow people to exercise their basic human rights and freedoms.

International Committee of the Red Cross

The International Committee of the Red Cross is the custodian of the Geneva Conventions and works to hold armed actors accountable through dialogue and negotiation. If you want to improve the conduct of war, you may want to consider going to law school so that you can become qualified as a legal advisor or human rights attorney.

In my career, I was fortunate to serve as an advisor to the ICRC, strengthening the organization's relationship with

U.S. Government officials during a change in administration. Understanding how government works and how to influence decision makers to improve humanitarian policy is also an important skill set for addressing the root causes of conflict.

Civil-Military Relations

I have worked with the military on protecting civilians in war. I have done this by developing training scenarios that place military officers in situations where they have to distinguish between military targets and civilians in need of protection.

One of the training exercises I developed was a game of sorts, where we created virtual avatars for military officers to "play" humanitarian workers in an emergency setting. I did this so that the military could better understand how humanitarian agencies function, including the principles and standards under which they operate. Other trainings I've developed are conducted via "tabletop" exercises that place people into teams that are given specific tasks such as analyzing changing conditions in a warring country and developing strategies to minimize harm to civilians.

If you are working in conflict zones as a humanitarian, you will come into contact with police and military forces. Understanding the functions and roles of the security sector in relation to humanitarian work is something you can learn by conducting research and taking a Civil-Military Coordination course through the UN Office for the Coordination of Humanitarian Affairs (OCHA).[11]

---

[11]OCHA manages a website, *Relief Web*, which is a helpful resource for humanitarian information.

Peacebuilding

Within every war-torn nation, there are people working for peace. Numerous organizations work with local communities to address the social, economic, and political grievances that fuel conflict. These organizations can be local civil society networks or large international charities.

Some peacebuilding organizations specialize in engaging women in politics and decision making, which is an important step toward greater social cohesion within fractured societies. Even with concerted effort to establish a national government that includes women, Afghanistan has struggled for decades to accept central governing authorities over regional, tribal, and religious affiliations which fracture alliances, fuel instability, and sideline the role of women at the local level. Still, working toward women's political empowerment and participation in the economy is transformative work that offers hope to future generations.

Peacebuilding is an increasingly professional field, with specialized degree programs at the graduate level. The Alliance for Peacebuilding (AFP) and the Peace and Collaborative Development Network (PCDN) are helpful resources for more information on this field.

Fighting Poverty

Like war, poverty is another root cause of instability that leads people to leave their homes in search of a better life. Poverty is often a symptom of economic and social inequalities within society which allow some people to have more, while others suffer with less.

In Haiti, people live on merely **$2 a day**, with average earnings of $700 a year. Could you live on $700 a month, let alone a whole year? These meager resources result in impossible choices for ordinary people. These choices include having to decide between eating or sending your children to school, and whether to pay rent or get medical care. Imagine how a resource-constrained country like Haiti can cope when disaster strikes, such as the 2010 earthquake that demolished 250,000 homes and displaced over a million people. Or when Hurricane Matthew struck the coast in 2016, destroying 90% of the crops that produce food and killing most of the livestock that provided food and income for the people.

When my organization, *Protect the People*, assessed conditions of people affected by Hurricane Matthew, it became clear that the country needed important agricultural resources to cope with the shock of losing its food supply. First, it needed a seed bank so that crops could be replanted as soon as possible. Second, it needed a cadre of skilled farmers who could quickly replant as many hectares of land as possible. Third, it needed food aid because it had neither the first nor second requirement.

In our assessment of the affected area, we identified one local organization that had a seed bank. However, they worked with subsistence farmers at the household level, which kept families from going hungry but wasn't enough to put food back on the market. So, relief agencies kept importing food aid from China, which suppressed the local market.

Although we were not able to find a seed bank large enough to replant crops that would keep people from requiring emergency food aid, my organization made multiple presentations to donors and government officials in the capital. We worked alongside reputable farming associations to explain how long-term investments in agriculture would allow people to recover quicker the next time there was a disaster, fostering resilience and reducing dependency on foreign aid.

Good and Bad News

Conditions in countries like Afghanistan, Haiti, Sudan, and Ukraine can seem overwhelming. They lead people to stand back in frustration, saying that nothing can be done. Behind the big picture of each major conflict and disaster, there are individual people who are stuck in bad situations. Sometimes they need urgent medical care and basic humanitarian relief. Sometimes they need a way out of the place where they live. Working with such individuals and communities means that even small gestures of help can make all the difference.

In this chapter we have explored the entrenched, root causes that fuel instability in countries that need systematic change—changes that include inclusive political systems, good governance, social cohesion, and economic growth. While humanitarian aid does not offer solutions to these problems, the way that aid is conducted can support long-term stability if it is done in partnership with local officials and communities.

The bad news is that many people living in crisis are from countries that have experienced recurring shocks. Decades of instability due to war and chronic disaster have made solving "humanitarian" problems impossible without addressing root causes. This means that, as a humanitarian, you might become frustrated by seeing people experience the same types of hardship over and over again, no matter how much time and money you give to a problem.

The good news is that being a humanitarian doesn't mean you have to have a certain job or career path. To address the root causes of conflict and disaster, the world also needs professionals dedicated to strengthening institutions and systems that sustain human life.

There are many ways you can make a difference. You can work in a large-scale financial institution, like the World Bank, or work with a small NGO making loans to the rural poor. You can work for a government agency dispensing official loans to strengthen governance, telecommunications infrastructure, sanitation, and health care. You can also work with armed groups to apply legal standards that make war less deadly for civilian populations or advocate for refugees to be accepted into a new country they can call home.

There are many ways to apply yourself to the problems you see in the world. The world needs your creativity and ingenuity. Be willing to work on tough problems that require long-term solutions.

3

THE BEST WAY TO MAKE A DIFFERENCE

"If you do not know where you are going,
then any road will take you there."
Lewis Carroll

This book has shown you how you can help humanity. You may be wondering:

What is the best way to make a real difference?

Humanitarian relief offers people a lifeline. Yet, even if you are not going to become an aid worker, there are many ways to become involved. As you start to help, you realize that meeting people's immediate needs doesn't solve other problems they face. Providing relief does not address the root causes of conflict or reduce someone's vulnerability to the next disaster.

Everyone comes to inflection points, when they stand in the middle of the road and wonder—what should I do next? At these important moments, it's good to step back and consider your options.

You can play a number of roles that will help others and serve humanity. This book has discussed some of the problems you can address and there are others such as gross inequality that leads to poverty, hatred and racism, criminal justice reform, and other social justice issues.

Ultimately, **you are only one person**. As one person, you can do a lot, but you cannot achieve big goals if you go it alone. To make a big difference, you have to engage a broad network of stakeholders. First, you will have to decide what role you want to play. This role is likely to shift over time as your priorities and personal circumstances change.

Here are a few approaches to doing the work ahead, so you can see the full range of options available to you.

Field Operations

Being in the field is by far the best way to be with the people affected by crisis. When you go out on assignment to locations where people are in need, you are able to see the immediate impact of your actions. By assessing people's conditions, making project plans, and then implementing programs, you have daily satisfaction that you are meeting people's needs.

The **upside of field work** is being close to the action, being with people and working in teams. Oftentimes, in remote field locations you will work alongside dedicated colleagues who have to improvise and find creative ways of getting things done on a daily basis. By being in the field, you will gain critical experience that is a fundamental requirement to apply for other positions in the sector. Being part of an emergency response is an immediate form of street credibility. By sharing this experience with fellow relief workers, you will earn the legitimacy to do more work in the future.

There are also some **drawbacks to being in the field**. You often don't have enough resources to meet all the needs you see. Living in remote locations will also require personal sacrifice in terms of family life and physical comfort. Many remote sites are not family duty stations, so you tend to find relief workers who are young people (just starting out), older people with grown children, and people who are divorced or separated from their families. In remote locations, you are also more likely to experience challenges to your personal safety and physical well-being.

Here are some important factors to consider:

The first is the basic state of **your health**. It is not advisable to work in remote areas if you have a serious medical condition or disability, or other personal constraints that would make it difficult for you to live without clean water, electricity, a balanced diet, and access to medical care.

Another factor is your temperament. A colleague told me a story about a young man who was eager to work in Darfur, Sudan helping people affected by ethnic violence. But after five days of eating only rice and tomatoes and going without a shower, he broke down and asked to be transferred to a site where he could function. Some people can function in these remote areas, others cannot. Know your limits at the outset, and only accept assignments that are suitable for you.

Country and Regional Offices

Many humanitarian positions are based at country and regional headquarters. These locations tend to be in urban hubs such as Bangkok, Thailand; Amman, Jordan; Nairobi, Kenya; and San Jose, Costa Rica, among others.

These offices often have oversight of programs in multiple locations. In these offices, you have programmatic, administrative, or technical functions depending on your area of expertise.

Regional program managers monitor the implementation of projects in several countries, reviewing work plans and managing country teams. Technical experts in these offices provide guidance in specific sectors such as child protection, food security, and shelter and facilitate regional training that strengthens programs. They can also write reports on thematic areas requiring further advocacy with governments and donors, in coordination with the communications team and agency leadership.

Advantages of working in a regional office include having a more diverse perspective on the range of humanitarian activities happening in the area. The country teams represented in regional offices, your colleagues, will be professional staff who come into the office each day. These offices are based in cosmopolitan urban areas that also tend to be family-friendly, with numerous expat communities to tap into for making life-long friends. These locations also have more career options for partners and better schooling for children.

Disadvantages of being in a regional office include feeling distant from the field and the people you serve. It can also be frustrating for regional officers to be the "middleman" between field offices and headquarters, given that there are often competing demands for resources. Prioritization of efforts is difficult at every level of humanitarian work, but it is even harder when comparing the benefits of one program over another or one country over another. Regional offices tend to be at the center of these debates for attention and resources within an organization.

Headquarters (HQ)

Agency headquarters are the centers of decision-making and leadership. These are based in major hubs of humanitarian agencies such as Geneva, Switzerland or New York, United States along with London, England and Dubai, in the United Arab Emirates.

Headquarter offices consolidate an agency's core administrative functions and serve as a hub for communications and advocacy efforts. Here, leaders are trying to shape the humanitarian agenda globally by bringing attention to core problems faced by their field, country, and regional offices around the world.

Headquarters also focus on efforts to secure funding from donors. This includes traditional notions of fundraising from generating appeals and responding to requests for proposals to investing in alternative forms of financing that engage with corporate and individual donors.

An advantage of working at headquarters is having your finger on the pulse on what's going on globally. Within any headquarters, you have access to reports from all the teams in the field. This enables you to see the "big picture" of problems the agency is working to address, which enables people who focus on advocacy and communications to thrive. It is also essential to have good administrative staff at this level, including leadership, finance, and human resources. The senior team of any organization is also responsible for holding the organization accountable to meeting donor expectations and maintaining high standards of conduct and quality control.

Headquarter locations also tend to have the highest quality of life, in terms of financial compensation and housing options, as well as schools for children and work opportunities for other family members, although they also have a higher cost of living than other duty stations.

Disadvantages of working at headquarters include infighting for the prioritization of efforts, given budgetary constraints and communications efforts. Some people who have worked in the field for a long time enjoy the quality of life in these duty stations. Others may feel lost in administrative procedures and long meetings. Some people in headquarters feel too far removed from the people they are serving. However, these positions usually require frequent travel to the field to support other offices, which allows people to stay in touch with developments on the ground.

However, another drawback of working at headquarters is having to decide which programs receive more funding and which programs have to be closed. Sometimes good projects are shut down due to changes in donor priorities or the security situation, as well as other factors beyond the control of aid workers in the field. It can be frustrating for first responders to see a need, develop a program, and build a team only to close an office down a short time later due to insufficient funds or a decision from headquarters. This happens more often than people realize, so being flexible and remaining in good contact with your agency headquarters can help you stay ahead of such decisions.

Fieldwork vs. Office Settings

Regardless of what level you work at within an organization, you will need different skills working in an office than you do in a field setting.

In the field, you need to be flexible and creative, able to adjust to changing situations on the ground. You need to have an acute awareness of the relevant actors in your operational area so you can coordinate your actions with other agencies and maintain awareness of the security situation to keep your team safe. This often requires quick decision-making to achieve short-term results.

In an office, you need to apply a more measured, professional way of working that includes having patience with yourself and your colleagues. You also need to be capable of implementing procedures and processes to keep multiple programs on track according to the schedule of deliverables and outputs laid out in donor agreements. You will also need to prioritize efforts when competing demands and budgetary pressures require changes in approach. This means adjusting your mindset to plan for longer term needs and developing systemic approaches to problem-solving.

Non-Governmental Organizations (NGOs)

Many people start out in the humanitarian sector by working for nongovernmental organizations (NGOs). As a Program Officer or Program Manager for an NGO, you will be responsible for one or more projects in the field. This involves compiling reports from the field and traveling to monitor existing programs or conduct assessments to develop new programs. Program management positions also include tracking the program budget, with support from the finance team, and reviewing indicators as to whether program goals are being met in coordination with the monitoring, evaluation, and learning team.

NGOs come in all shapes and sizes; some are large, multi-billion-dollar organizations with a formidable presence on the ground, and others are nimble, low-budget operations getting by with small teams of people. Instead of trying to do everything, most NGOs work to streamline efforts and specialize in particular types of programming. For example, the UK charity Oxfam specializes in water and sanitation, while Save the Children focuses on child-friendly programming, and organizations like World Vision tend to concentrate their efforts on child protection and food security.

Major **advantages** of working for NGOs include working directly with affected populations and gaining critical experience. You may also have fewer resources to do the work, which will help you get creative and try new ideas. One seasoned aid worker told me that working for NGOs helped him to "get scrappy" by working with what he had. This ability to be adaptive and flexible in the work is an incredibly helpful skill.

Disadvantages of working for NGOs tend to be limited job security due to shifting annual budgets which drive short-term contracting mechanisms. If you want to work for an NGO, it's important to conduct research on who is doing what, where, and in which sector. You can do much of this research online, through portals such as Relief Web, the UN Office for the Coordination of Humanitarian Affairs (OCHA), and other regional and country-specific networking sites. It's also important to ask NGOs about their budget and donor commitment to your particular position or project so you can plan how long you will be there.

Government Agencies

Working for a government agency that provides Official Development Assistance (ODA) in the form of grants and cooperative agreements is another option. These positions are great for someone who is starting out and who desire the stability of a long-term career. Organizations such as the UK Department for International Development (DFID) and U.S. Agency for International Development (USAID) have entry-level positions where you can get specialized training in a particular field. These positions require a university degree, international experience (which you can meet through volunteering and internships), and foreign language skills.

Job security and longevity is an **advantage** of working for the government. In addition, government agencies have access to information that provides a "big picture" perspective to what is going on in a given area. Unfortunately, this knowledge also brings regulations and security protocols which are less tolerant of risk. Thus, a **disadvantage** is that government workers tend to feel frustrated by all the bureaucracy, especially travel rules that limit their ability to access people and programs. Many government workers depend on intermediaries such as local and international NGOs to implement and report on the work that they fund or support.

Donors and Philanthropy

While traditional donors are comprised of official government agencies, an array of private foundations and companies contribute to humanitarian operations. Working as a Program Officer for a philanthropic foundation or donor can be very exciting and fulfilling, allowing you to network with a wide range of NGOs and human rights organizations.

One **advantage** of being a Program Officer is that donors do not necessarily expect you to be an expert in the field. In fact, young people with a Master's in Business Administration (MBA) and other technical degrees beyond the field of International

Relations are highly sought after by the private sector. Donors expect Program Officers to be decisive, capable of evaluating numerous proposals and arguing for where to make the best investment. This includes forming relationships with agencies of interest to the donor and weighing the pros and cons of providing funding to which agency, where, and for how long. This is part of a decision-making process—comparing where a certain amount of funds will have the greatest impact and comparing the strengths and weakness of agencies doing similar work. Many donor program officers end up taking leadership positions in NGOs because they know how to attract and maintain a network of fundraising prospects.

While the rules that govern travel and risk assessments for philanthropic entities vary, one potential **disadvantage** of working for a foundation could be restrictions from traveling to the field. Some donors enjoy going on trips to see the work they support firsthand, others do not. Donors also have special interests and are less focused on making decisions based on need. Make sure to do your homework about how the foundation operates and how it measures success so you can be sure a philanthropic role is right for you.

United Nations (UN) and Multilateral Agencies

When you're first starting out, working for the United Nations is a lofty goal, but there are numerous ways of going about "getting in." First, if you are looking for an entry-level position, there are entrance exams given twice a year at UN headquarters around the world. These exams are not well-advertised, so you have to research when they are being offered. Once the UN grades your skill level, you can be placed in an assignment.

Entry-level positions in the UN also require an undergraduate degree, international experience, and fluency in one or more UN languages. There are five official UN languages: English, Spanish, French, Arabic, and Mandarin. Many people will tell you that to be competitive in the UN, you have to speak two or three of these languages. Therefore, it is imperative that you spend time overseas to achieve professional fluency in the language prior to competing for a UN post. Taking language classes and knowing a few words to hold a basic conversation will not be enough to pass the language exam.

Another way to get into the UN is to apply for Junior Professional Officer (JPO) positions, many of which are sponsored by the nations. Check with the foreign ministry of your country or the U.S. State Department to see which JPO positions are open to your nationality. These positions are more formal than an internship. They offer time-limited roles with modest pay as a way of getting into the system and gaining experience. Becoming a United Nations Volunteer (UNV) is another way for young professionals to get into the system.

In order to hold a more senior position within a UN agency, you will need considerable technical expertise and more than ten years of experience overseas. Many senior management positions within the UN also require, implicitly or explicitly, the backing of your national government. Although UN positions are not political appointments per se, they are representative posts where your nationality and your network matter as much as the skills you bring to the role.

If these options don't seem open to you, take heart. You can work for an NGO or donor for many years and network your way into a UN position if that is your ultimate goal. However, be aware that as you gain more experience in the work, you will be competing for positions with people who also have considerable overseas experience. Preference is often given to internal candidates that have served in the respective agency for many years, making it harder to break in.

The upside of working for the UN and other multilateral agencies, like the European Union, is working closely with representatives of different countries to achieve your mission. Significant milestones for humanity are reached when nations work together. For example, the UN negotiates international agreements on human rights, climate change, migration, and peacekeeping missions. You will also get to work in a dynamic, multi-cultural environment where you can use political and diplomatic skills. Having personal charisma and the ability to persuade others is a critical skillset for this work. Another **advantage** is that the UN pays well and offers substantial benefits.

Drawbacks to this work include having to navigate a complex bureaucracy, which often emphasizes process and procedures over results. Because the UN represents its member states, the organization can be overtly political, selecting people based on networks rather than merit.

Some people who work for the UN are frustrated that the organization does not live up to its goals, placing the interests of member states above vulnerable populations who need assistance and protection from human rights abuses. Member states that control decisions in the Security Council include countries that block votes and resolutions that could help people, such as authorizing cross-border humanitarian assistance for Syria or investigating crimes against humanity in Darfur, for example.

That is why achieving results for humanity includes political advocacy, which is also known as humanitarian diplomacy.

Policy and Advocacy

Because there are so many gaps between what people need and the political will to meet those needs, **advocacy is critical to humanitarian work.**

Some humanitarian advocates argue for more funding for a particular crisis, showing the gap between funding appeals and money raised. Others work to elevate the human stories and faces behind those appeals, raising public awareness through various communications channels. Advocacy can also be more formal, such as taking up a legal case against a particular government for crimes against humanity.

The term *"humanitarian diplomacy"* is used to describe the process of convincing governments to act in the best interest of humanity. This is done at the field, country, and multi-lateral level with governments or groups of nations at the UN.

Just as you cannot expect to achieve results as one person alone, any one nation cannot convince other countries to change their position without coming together in common cause. This is why the UN Security Council authorizes sanctions against nations that have acted irresponsibly against international laws and norms. At the UN, you also find "Groups of Friends" comprised of nations working on a particular problem set, from peacekeeping and protecting civilians to climate change.

There are numerous ways you can join these advocacy efforts. You can start today by writing an editorial or posting about one of the needs described in this book. You can also meet with your local or national representatives to address a need in your community. You could also pursue a career in the legal field, representing individuals and groups of people in just causes.

Advocating for people in need is critical to keeping a crisis on the minds of donor governments. Convincing those in authority to use their decision-making power to help others can create tangible benefits for many people.

Governments also set standards for the protection of vulnerable people, provide resources for humanitarian operations, give direction to military command structures, and put pressure on authorities to take specific actions.

This work often requires a legal background, public speaking, and good writing skills. To be effective, you will need to influence others. You will also need to develop and maintain an extensive network of people to help you get things done.

The upside of advocacy work includes having a greater impact on people when you do achieve success. For example, as the Director of Government Relations for an NGO, I drafted amendments to legislation that provided millions of dollars in funding for refugees and negotiated an agreement that reunited thousands of families separated by war. These were rewarding accomplishments that had a great impact.

Drawbacks of working in the political realm include the feeling of swimming against the tide, especially when you are trying to influence government officials that don't care about people's needs. When governments fail to protect the people, humanitarian agencies are there to clean up the mess. But it would be much better if authorities acted responsibly to resolve disputes and prevent disasters before a situation becomes catastrophic.

More Ways to Make a Difference

Even if you are not in an international line of work, organizations need your support to volunteer, donate, and advocate with them. As you get more involved, also consider joining the board of a charitable group. Nonprofits in your community need leaders who are willing to step up by giving more, doing more, and speaking up for their cause. Board members go the extra mile by developing strategic plans, leading fundraising campaigns, and representing the organization to donors. Check out online portals such as Idealist, Board Source, and the United Way for opportunities to serve.

4

ACHIEVING YOUR VISION

Change is Possible

In your life, you are going to need a vision to guide you along the way. As you try to help people, you will realize that your vision goes beyond yourself. You are trying to do things beyond what many hope to achieve. This life is not about having a bigger house and a better car. It is not about climbing the corporate ladder and retiring well. Your friends and family may think your desire to help people is a worthwhile pursuit but an unachievable goal. They may tell you the world is messed up beyond repair. They may ask,

What can you possibly hope to accomplish in such a messed-up world?

You can start by having a realistic vision about what one person can achieve. Believe in yourself and what is possible. Put your whole self into this work—your time and your money, even your heart. In this chapter, I'm going to outline what you can reasonably expect from a lifetime of helping.

Although you will come up against tough challenges, you will see changes for the better in people's lives. This change is evident at four levels:

1. Individual
2. Group
3. Community
4. Country

Global, life-changing work is out there for you to accomplish. Understanding how change happens will enable you to be patient as you work toward your vision. Having realistic expectations of what you can achieve will also help you to be patient with others who may not share your vision. This chapter is going to give you examples from the transformations I have seen with my own eyes of the change that is possible.

When I graduated from Oxford University, I had the honor of walking down the aisle of the Sheldonian Theatre, where literary greats like C.S. Lewis, who wrote *The Lion, Witch and the Wardrobe* among other great works, and J.R.R. Tolkien, who wrote *The Lord of the Rings*, also graduated and people who invented languages and curated diseases had gone before me. I was overcome by a feeling of being adopted into a society of men and women who had done great things. As I received my degree, I heard an inner whisper:

The greatest things to be done for mankind have yet to be accomplished.

That's what I wanted more than anything. *I wanted to do great things*. I have come to learn that *the greatest contribution you can make is to give yourself*. In this chapter we will see all the accomplishments that are possible once you do.

You can help people overcome overwhelming odds. By changing conditions that were once dire, you can empower people to change their lives. Through humanitarian programs, children once orphaned by war are placed in new families. Refugees displaced by conflict are finding new, permanent homes. Communities affected by disease are restoring health by preventing the spread of deadly infections. Countries are being transformed by changes in government and economic policy that are lifting people out of poverty.

Standing by Your Principles

No matter what level of change you try to pursue, you are going to need the strength of character to stay the course when things get hard. I want to give you practical examples that will encourage you as you go about the business of helping. I also want to tell you that one of the most powerful aspects of believing in humanity is *the strength of your convictions.*

In an earlier chapter, I shared that humanitarians operate under principles established by the international movement of the Red Cross. These principles include *humanity, impartiality, neutrality, independence, voluntary service, unity, and universality.* Each principle is important because it helps answer the question of why and how we do the work; we do it because we value humanity and we seek to help those who are suffering regardless of the person's origin or opinion. As I discussed earlier, humanitarians care for people indiscriminately, regardless of their position, place, race, ethnicity, nationality, gender, sexual preference, religion, etc.

Humanitarians help people far beyond the programs they implement. You can strengthen others with *the power of your ideals,* by the confidence that we are on a noble and important mission which requires partnership with people on the ground. We act in faith each time we get on a plane to join a crisis response team—faith that when we hit the ground, there will be people of goodwill on the other side who will work with us as a united team in an effort to save lives.

If you chose to serve others, you will be further strengthened by *the power of your ideas.* Humanitarians share a mindset that humanity is good and that ultimately, goodwill prevails in the end. We have faith in humanity itself, being sure that a better world is available to those who seek it. We put our lives on the line for this vision, that people everywhere should live in freedom and with dignity: free from fear and free from want, free to live in peace and in relative prosperity.[12] We do this because we know that once people are able to live freely, they contribute to a better world for everyone.

Forming Your Vision

Humanitarians share a common purpose to alleviate suffering. You will also need a personal vision to guide you on your path. Set personal goals for yourself in life.

It's a big world out there, and I want you to keep going when you realize that tough problems are at the root of human suffering. Even when there aren't *"quick fixes"* to a problem, do what you can each day. Even as you keep the bigger picture in mind, focus on what you can accomplish as one person. When you start to achieve small levels of change, you will see how even bigger changes happen.

Having a personal vision to start out with will carry you through when you don't see results right away. Although every organization you work for will have its own vision statement, you should also have a personal statement to guide your work. To develop your vision statement, ask yourself a few important questions:

1. What is motivating me to do this work?
2. Am I the right person to do this work?

---

[12]U.S. President Franklin Roosevelt gave the "Four Freedoms" speech before Congress in 1941, stating that people everywhere should have freedom of religion and speech, freedom from fear, and freedom from want.

3. What problem am I trying to address?
4. What solution am I trying to achieve?
5. How will things change as a result of my success?

For example, when I was starting out, I chose this statement to guide me:

Stand in the gap.

Standing in the gap meant I wanted to work where people had unmet needs. I didn't want to work in situations that were already nice and neat. I wanted to fix the hard problems and go to the tough places where I was needed. I wanted to be part of the solution by addressing problems head on.

As you will see later, my sense of purpose changed as a result of Hurricane Katrina, which became a watershed moment for me when I saw that people's needs were going unmet in my own home country. Then my statement changed to:

Protect the people.

After Hurricane Katrina, when I saw the United States was prioritizing the rebuilding of infrastructure above saving people's lives, I shifted my focus to advocating for the protection of people. I eventually formed an organization called *Protect the People (PTP)* which developed a formal vision statement to address the safety, dignity, and well-being of people affected by crisis.

When I formed Protect the People, a number of wealthy donors asked me: who are you protecting exactly? I tried to explain to them what it meant to be a vulnerable person in crisis and that protection didn't mean guarding people with weapons. It meant offering people dignity and rights and speaking out on their behalf.

However, when I traveled to a disaster recovery conference in New Orleans, I stayed at a hotel right across from the Convention Center where many people died as a result of the storm. When the women at the front desk saw my business card with the Protect the People logo, they gasped and said, *"You are for us."* That was one of the best moments of my life.

Understanding how small steps are helping you achieve a bigger vision will help you stay focused when the path seems long and change is hard to come by. It's important to see points of progress along the path to greater goals. There are numerous ways of measuring your own personal effectiveness. There are also several ways to achieve change at the individual, group, community, and country level.

The humanitarian sector needs *powerful individuals and powerful institutions* to make sustained improvements in people's lives. Earlier in my career, I was suspect of large institutions and bureaucracies. They seemed slow to function, reluctant to make decisions, and averse to taking quick action. Over time I came to realize that without strong institutions to administer services, adjudicate justice, provide security, and have a functioning government, systems will fail the people. Good governance and institution building are at the heart of protecting human rights, achieving dignity, and ensuring sustainable development.

Measuring Impact

Setting a vision is one thing; knowing the steps to reach it is another. Measuring your impact is important to keeping yourself focused, motivated, and moving forward. We will discuss the kind of change you can expect to see as a result of your efforts later in this chapter. First, you should know there is an entire discipline focused on monitoring, evaluation, and learning that helps measure the impact of humanitarian and development programs.

Nonprofit organizations measure program effectiveness by counting the number of clients they serve. This keeps agencies accountable to donors about the amount of money they spend per person.

When you start out in this line of work, you will compile detailed reports about how many people you helped and how your work has changed lives. When you are assigned to a new team, you can ask to see the monthly or annual reports that show how the organization measures its impact. These reports give you a good idea of the scope of an agency's work in a specific country or sector.

Today, there are complex models for measuring effectiveness that include the inputs and outputs for each program activity, such as whether teaching people to wash their hands results in a decrease in disease, whether supplemental feeding programs result in reduced rates of malnutrition, or whether providing information to refugees about conditions in their country improves the rate of people who return home.

Organizations use logical frameworks to track these inputs and outputs, with each activity or objective guided by theories of change about what causes impact. In addition, there are standard measurements of performance and indicators of effectiveness for every sector as well as other industry standards that guide ethical research and government funding. There's also increasing emphasis on learning and innovation to help achieve sustainable results that can be scaled. That brings us to the question:

What changes can you make, as one person?

Four Levels of Change

There are four levels of change you can expect to see by helping people:

1. First, you will see changes in **individual lives.** You will be motivated by knowing that each day, you are increasing the number of people being reached. Helping one person can change the world. In the course of your normal life, wherever you are, look for that person who has a need. Be willing to serve as a lifeline to that person. If you pursue a humanitarian career, you will be assisting hundreds of thousands of people by starting with one.

2. Second, you will increase opportunities for **entire groups** of people to have a better life. You can change conditions for a group of people by focusing your efforts on targeted interventions to change their living conditions. I have seen this firsthand working with refugees in Africa and Asia. I have also seen changes in specific demographics of people, such as improving women's lives in Afghanistan, reducing the vulnerability of children in Thailand, and providing opportunity to farmers in Haiti.

3. Third, you will also see **communities transformed.** When people work together as a team, they can do amazing things. You can be a catalyst that inspires people to change their own lives, together in community. I can't wait to tell you how women in Zambia stopped the spread of HIV/AIDS in their community. When a committed group of people have a shared sense of purpose to pursue a common vision, they can do anything.

4. Fourth, you will see **countries rebuild**. It may not make the headlines, but at the national level, entire countries have been transformed. Several countries have experienced successful transitions from crisis to stability. Nations at war make the transition to peace after periods of turmoil. When people can rebuild their lives in peace, it is an indicator that the country is on a path to stability.

When individual needs are met, groups are empowered, and communities are united, the nation is healed.

Paths to Progress

Whether you are helping a person, a group, a community, or a country, your efforts are part of the bigger picture of human progress. Let me show you how this is accomplished.

On my first assignment, I collected and analyzed reports from relief teams throughout the African continent. I worked for World Vision, a relief agency that focuses on children in crisis. In the 1990s, one of the toughest places to help children was in Rwanda. The 1994 genocide, which killed 800,000 people in 100 days, resulted in 100,000 children without parents.

In the aftermath of mass killings, there were not enough adults to care for all the children left behind. World Vision recognized the high number of child-headed households and started programs to help older children care for their younger siblings. Relief teams put support mechanisms in place for childcare givers, such as identifying adult foster parents to pay for school fees so children could continue their education. They also established vocational training schools for older children to earn an income.

World Vision programs in Rwanda started by assessing the needs of each child, like Alphonsina, who, at only 15 years old, was responsible for caring for her four younger brothers and growing crops to feed the family. With the support of World Vision, she was able to continue her schooling and receive the support of caring adults in her community.[13]

By reporting on the situation of children like Alphonsina, the World Vision regional office in South Africa where I worked was able to get support from donors to expand services, reaching vulnerable children across Rwanda. Bringing attention to a problem can increase the funding for agencies to reach more people, impacting lives and changing hard circumstances.

Farmers in Haiti

When my organization, Protect the People, started assessing needs in Haiti after the 2010 earthquake, we quickly realized that supporting agricultural communities was key to reducing dependency on food aid. We also discovered that rural farmers did not access formal banking and could not get the working capital necessary to buy land or the farming inputs such as seed, fertilizer, and irrigation systems that increase crop yield and lead to a good harvest.

Through a partnership with the Center for Global Development, we developed a mechanism for Haitian farmers to temporarily work on farms in the United States, earning up to 28-times their meager annual income of $700 in Haiti.

---

[13]Vanessa Veck with *The New York Times* has documented World Vision Rwanda's work with children orphaned by the genocide in this photo documentary, 1999. http://movies2.nytimes.com/library/world/africa/index-rwanda-children.html

The first group of farmers to participate in the program were hand-selected after rigorous vetting mechanisms. This was critical to ensuring that each person would utilize the income they earned to its maximum benefit to increase food security in Haiti.

We measured the program's progress by the amount of income each farmer earned. We also carefully evaluated what each person did with the additional income. With the money they earned, farmers created new businesses, hired workers, purchased land, built new homes, and paid their children's school fees.

What I didn't expect was the indelible impact the program made on the lives of each individual farmer. One man told me,

"This program has given me the confidence that I can do anything."

Another beneficiary said that the program gave him a new family among the other farmers who participated. The best result I heard was,

"This project made me believe in myself. Now I know that I am greater than my circumstances."

In the midst of crises, humanitarian programs can transform people's lives. When individuals feel like they have lost everything, you can be the person who helps them recover. Your efforts can restore hope to people who would otherwise be hopeless.

Here's another key point to remember. Don't be overwhelmed even when the situation seems overwhelming. People are incredibly adaptive and responsive. Sometimes all they need in order to rebuild is a helping hand. You can be the person who is there for others in a time of need.

Working with refugees has shown me how entire groups of people rebuild their lives. Earlier, I mentioned that living in camps is not the best place for refugees because they can become dependent on aid. One of these solutions is returning home to their country of origin. Voluntary repatriation involves a number of steps, depending on the relationship between the refugees and their home country. Here's how a few different groups of refugees have found a permanent home.

Refugees from Mauritania

When I started counting the number of Mauritanian refugees in Senegal as part of the census, the Government of Mauritania did not want the refugees to come back. The same government that expelled them because of their dark skin, calling them "Africans," not Arabs, took land away from black farmers. Despite the government's opposition to them, these farmers wanted to go back because relief agencies were cutting their food rations. They wanted to go home and grow their own food.

Three years after the census was completed, with 600,000 refugees counted, a new government was elected in Mauritania. The new leadership no longer saw the country as being divided between its black Sub-Saharan and white Arab identity. The refugees were allowed to return home. The census I worked on prepared the way for the group's organized return and recognized individual claims for property restitution and the resumption of citizenship rights.

Although my work was only a small part of the bigger picture, I felt that I was part of the refugees' success story. Although I was not there when they crossed the border back to their country, I was with them in spirit, celebrating the end of their long journey. They were going home, and my work helped prepare the way for their arrival.

Civilians in Afghanistan

I also helped internally displaced people (IDPs) in southern Afghanistan, working with an NGO and the UN High Commissioner for Refugees. In 2002, Afghan refugees were returning from Pakistan only to find out that fighting between the Taliban and U.S. forces inside the country made it difficult to fully return to their place of origin. My team's task was to assist and provide protection to 500,000 people trapped by fighting along the border of Afghanistan and Pakistan.

The United Nations was eager to relocate people away from the border of Pakistan since active fighting in the area made civilians vulnerable to military strikes. After identifying safer locations to the interior of the country and getting permission to use land for new settlements, we moved people away from the border.

However, many civilians were reluctant to leave the border zone, which was a good area to engage in commercial trade. We could only offer civilians a partial solution to their many challenges. We could provide them with a safer place to live, where they could wait out the fighting, but we couldn't guarantee that they would have access to trade that provided the income they needed to survive.

Caring for One Another

One day, after trying to move as many people as possible away from the border, I went back to my office in Kandahar to prepare a report about the number of people we relocated to safety. Sitting down at my desk, I realized I was dusty and dirty as I closed out the day. I was tempted to throw up my hands in discouragement, thinking about the number of people who still needed a safe place to go. Those who remained along the border were likely to become "collateral damage" as military operations increased the number of aerial raids.

Then, I looked out the window. My translator was sitting outside with our driver, teaching him how to read. Watching the two men go over each word in a book, I felt a deep sense of pride. They didn't need to be in the office. Everyone had gone home for the day.

Days earlier, when I was training the team for cross-border operations, my translator came up to me with a message from the group. Looking aside, he whispered to me.

"Ms. Sarah," he said, trying to get my attention.

"We all decided; you care too much. Try to care less, and things will go better for you." Then he laughed and walked away.

In a country with a literacy rate of 30%, here were two men who stayed late in the office to help each other. I taught them to look out for the needs of others, and in return, they began looking out for each other. They also wanted a better life for themselves.

I often felt that the best thing I did in Afghanistan was build a team of people who knew how to assess needs in their own community. As I looked at the two men reading together, I knew that I had taught them something of immeasurable value: new ways to care for one another.

Refugees from Vietnam

It's not easy to find a permanent solution for an entire group of refugees, but when Vietnamese refugees became stranded in the Philippines, a special initiative made it possible to resettle all 2,000 people who were forgotten after the Vietnam War. Working with a charismatic friend from Oxford, I helped document and present the cases of each stranded person to countries that would consider them for resettlement on a humanitarian basis.

Many of the Vietnamese refugees were women and children whose husbands and fathers were rescued at sea by U.S. warships. During a conflict, men often leave home first while the women stay behind to care for older relatives. Women were left behind as the men sought safety elsewhere. When the war ended and the women tried to leave the country with their children, U.S. ships were no longer at sea. Thus, the boats with women and children landed on remote islands that were not capable of processing their refugee claims or issuing identity documents. They became de facto stateless persons.

My colleague and I presented the group's case to the United States Government. We asked the group to be considered for the refugee resettlement program. We found sympathetic officials in the White House, one of whom had a Vietnamese roommate in college. We also received support from the late Senator John McCain who was a Prisoner of War in Vietnam. After all this time when everyone thought the war had ended, he was astonished to hear that refugees were still stuck on remote islands.

We negotiated an agreement with the U.S. State Department to accept all 2,000 people as a group for admission to the refugee resettlement program. Being part of a permanent solution to reunify these families was incredibly rewarding. This time, I was there at the airport in Manila to see the first refugee families leave for the United States. It was a happy "case closed."

Years later, when Typhoon Haiyan hit the Philippines, the refugees we resettled donated $500,000 to relief efforts. That's the result of helping a determined group of people. When refugees have an opportunity to thrive, they become productive members of society who give back to others. What a great contribution.

As you can see, when you assist individuals and groups, you are really touching the lives of entire communities.

Chikumbuso

In Africa, nothing has devastated communities more than the HIV/AIDS crisis, which has affected millions of people. In the course of my work, I've had the opportunity to serve on the board of several organizations, including a women's cooperative in Zambia called Chikumbuso, which means "remembering to do for others." One of my favorite examples of community change comes from the amazing women there, living in the township of Ngombe outside the capital city of Lusaka.

When my friend relocated to Zambia with her husband, she was looking for a way to get involved in the community. One day, she met a widow who was caring for six children orphaned by HIV/AIDS. The woman was hungry, so she brought her some *mealie meal*, a popular food staple in Zambia, and asked the woman to share her story. The widow told her that many women were caring for children orphaned by the disease. They gathered together a group of seven widows and began to address needs in the community, such as how to afford school fees for the many children left behind.

Even though the need was great, my friend did not look away. As a former teacher, she started a class for the children, which became an accredited primary school. She also started widow and grandmother circles where women could offer each other mutual support.

One day, the conversation focused on how they could generate income. The women decided to crochet recycled plastic bags into colorful purses to sell at the local market. The bags became so popular they decided to pool their profits together in a bank, saving a portion of the proceeds from each bag they sold to fund community projects. They also raised money from generous donors in the United States.

Buying the Brothel

When the women raised enough money to consider making a large purchase, they were united in their decision about what to buy. They wanted to address the source of their problems, to get at what was causing HIV infections in the first place. The organization decided to buy the brothel at the center of town. The men who visited the brothel would go there to drink, buy drugs, and find prostitutes. Then they went home to sleep with their wives, spreading HIV/AIDS, which killed many adults in their community. The women saw the brothel as a direct threat to their health.

The women bought the brothel with the help of a generous donor and cleaned it up, painted it, and turned it into a community center where children could play. They turned what was once a symbol of darkness into a beacon of light, inviting everyone in the community to come and use the facility.

Chikumbuso provides an education for 500 children in grades K-7 and is supporting 78 college students. Many of these children were orphans and street children with no hope of ever going to school. The women of Ngombe continue to advance their earnings by investing in real estate and other small business ventures. Their confidence in the future has transformed lives.

That's the transformative power of community. *The people you help are not helpless. They can be powerful agents of change.* That's how empowerment works. Chikumbuso could measure its impact by the amount of proceeds from the bags they sell or by the number of children now in school, but their work has an immeasurable impact: women who are taking control of their own destiny.

Transformations

Although the news makes it seem as if there is a continuous cycle of global chaos, wars do end, and countries are transformed by people working for peace.

Rwanda, a country once torn apart by ethnic cleansing, has served as a model for reconciliation and development. In the last ten years, 1 million people in this east African nation have risen out of poverty. This has been achieved through investments in agriculture, which have increased crop yields and multiplied rural incomes. Rwanda also banned plastic bags and instituted a national clean-up day called *Umuganda*, which means "coming together for a common purpose." On the last Saturday of each month, every Rwandan in the nation is required to take part in the national cleanup effort, which is a source of unity and pride.

Other African countries have successfully resolved conflicts by reforming their national armies. In Burundi and the Central African Republic, efforts to integrate different ethnic groups and warring factions into a unified army has been a core aspect of negotiated peace agreements that have reduced violence.

United Nations peacekeeping forces have successfully separated armed groups and improved security in Liberia and Sierra Leone, countries once torn apart by violence. National leaders committed to reconciliation are working through regional bodies like the African Union to bring peace to other nations, including Sudan and South Sudan.

Elsewhere in Asia, Sri Lanka is now at peace after 25 years of civil war between the government and the Tamil Tigers, a rebel group. Nepal was also torn apart by a decade of civil war during the Maoist Revolution, then signed a peace agreement in 2006 which ended the armed conflict.

These stories of hope remind us that countries can change course. While scholars continue to study what brings about conflict termination and an end to war, we know that it takes a few key ingredients such as political leadership, international pressure, and localized efforts that include the participation of women and young people.[14] *Humanitarian agencies that*

---

[14]For more information about trends in global conflict, see the Peace Research Institute of Oslo (PRIO) in Norway and the Uppsala Conflict Data Program (UCDP) in Sweden.

relieve the suffering of people in conflict are critical enablers of this peace by ensuring that people are capable of contributing to the future of the nation.

Disaster Risk Reduction

Like countries where latent conflicts are prone to arise, some nations—because of their location and environment—are more likely than others to experience natural disasters. Yet, an increase in disaster risk reduction planning is leading to better coping mechanisms to these shocks. This leads to resilience, improving adaptation to withstand a series of shocks over a period of time.

For example, the nation of Haiti, located in the heart of the Caribbean, is prone to hurricanes and earthquakes. Preparing for these frequent shocks would be easier if the government functioned with greater transparency and people had the personal finances to fortify their dwellings.

In the semi-desert land of Somalia, only 13% of the land is arable, which makes it prone to drought and flooding. The country depends on an inconsistent rainy season for both agricultural production and animal husbandry. Given that the country is divided by clan and state territories with varying degrees of autonomy, the central government has limited means to address these and other national threats.

Even in the United States, the intensification of weather patterns has led to wide-scale destruction along the Gulf Coast, Florida Keys, and in Puerto Rico. Major storms like Hurricane Katrina and Hurricane Maria killed thousands of people and resulted in billions of dollars in damage to critical infrastructure. Although the U.S. has the financial means to recover from major events, officials struggle to effectively respond to people whose lives are disrupted by natural disasters.

The good news about disaster reduction efforts is that vulnerable countries are becoming increasingly aware of the risks they face and are taking active measures to build resilience. Since Hurricane Katrina, the U.S. government has stockpiled critical supplies throughout the country, including portable drinking water and shelters, in the event of a disaster. Haiti has strengthened its Department of Civil Protection which oversees its local response framework, providing communities with early warning before a disaster strikes. Despite institutional challenges in Somalia, international agencies are working alongside the central government to predict rainfall patterns that serve as early warning indicators for drought and flooding.

Even in seemingly intractable conflicts and disaster-prone countries, there is always something you can do to reduce the vulnerability of people and nations. There are ways to develop strategies that mitigate risk and reduce exposure to harm. Although you may hear commentary on the news saying this or that country has always been a problem and solutions are impossible, don't believe everything you hear. What people mean to say is that they don't understand the complexity of the problem and, therefore, do not know what to do about it.

Even in the worst circumstances, there is always something you can do. There is no place on earth where people have stopped trying to live a better life for themselves and their children. Being a humanitarian gives you a front row seat to this transformation at all levels of change. By learning about people and places affected by crisis, you can better understand the problems people face and work toward solutions.

Delivering on big, world-changing ideas is not only difficult for individuals, but it is also a challenge for nations as they seek to influence the behavior of other countries. Solutions imposed from the outside looking in, by foreigners who do not have ownership over the end result, are prone to failure due to misunderstanding the problem and applying the wrong solutions. Therefore, whether you become a university professor or a Prime Minister, having humility and listening to other perspectives will help you find local solutions to big, global problems.

The Big Picture

If you haven't seen the big picture yet, here's an important take-away. While you can change the world as one person, *helping people is not a go-it-alone business.* You need to join a good organization and be part of a committed team of people to make a difference.

In the same way that individuals in crisis need the help of a supportive community, countries cannot always rescue themselves from a crisis. When countries are faced with overwhelming challenges, there is a need for an international response. When war and disaster strike, countries need help to manage the crisis and make the transition to normalcy.

The world is made up of 7.7 billion people. Despite the bad news you might hear, progress is happening at the global level. For example, less than 10% of the world's population lives in poverty today as opposed to thirty years ago. In 1990, 36% of the world's population lived on less than $1.90 a day, which is the measurement of extreme poverty used by the World Bank.

This global progress is not the result of isolated action. It's the result of millions of small steps that people like you and I take to make a better world. It's also the result of political and financial institutions working together to achieve systemic progress. Individuals and institutions are needed to achieve sustainable progress on a global scale.

Achieving a vision for humanity requires recognizing that human progress is an endless continuum of change. Each of us is a part of achieving a bigger picture. We will not achieve our vision alone, and we may not achieve everything we set out to accomplish in our lifetime. Yet, working toward progress is the only answer.

As you think about your role in the world, remember that you are only one person, but you can make a huge difference. *How* you make that difference often depends on your ability to bring other people along, to cast a vision that people want to follow, and to carry through on your ability to deliver results. You cannot succeed alone. But you will succeed if you join a good team, contribute to enduring institutions, and stay the course.

Imagine what you can accomplish by taking a small step forward. Make a personal vision statement to guide your path. Join the global community of people working to make the world a better place.

Remember, every effort you make counts.
Are you ready to take the next step?

5

BE PREPARED FOR OBSTACLES

What you want is to live in a better world. Making things better involves taking risks. This chapter is going to help you figure out how to take calculated risks and how to stay safe while you're out there changing lives.

Overcoming the kind of big challenges discussed in the previous chapter is difficult, for sure. Coming up against challenges to your personal health and safety can be even tougher. By going beyond your comfort zone, you are going to encounter people and places that are unstable. The same threat that disrupts lives and sends countries into chaos can also become a threat to you personally.

When you are faced with a threat to your safety, who doesn't want to retreat? **This chapter is meant to prepare you for the challenges you will face while trying to help people.** Frankly, what I write here is a bit dire, but I want you to be ready.

I'll share some of the challenges that I and others have faced, including being held hostage and nearly being killed in a car accident. In addition to these events, other challenges such as getting sick from food and water-borne diseases can also upend your mission. Ultimately, you need to be prepared for each and every situation. What I'm going to tell you will help you prepare for your assignment.

More Than I Bargained For

When you set out to do a good thing, you may face opposition where you least expect it. The people you want to help might have their own ideas about why you are there. They may suspect you and test your motives. Your beneficiaries and clients will have their own interests. People may want things from you that have nothing to do with your mission. I learned this the hard way in West Africa.

The story I'm about to share has some humorous elements, but it really wasn't funny. I wasn't a professional quite yet; I was studying abroad during my junior year of college. I was naïve about a few things back then.

I chose to study in Senegal, West Africa, where I could study in the French language at a local university and do an independent project working with refugees. The United Nations had a regional office in the capital city of Dakar. When I first met with UN officials to discuss internship opportunities, they suggested I work with a human rights organization working in refugee camps along the border with Mauritania. The group was conducting a census of the population to verify the amount of aid needed in the area and to negotiate the return of Mauritanian refugees who wanted to reclaim their land. After meeting with the leader of the human rights group, I made plans to travel with him to remote areas of the border.

Despite making well-thought-out plans to meet up with the human rights group, we got separated on the road. Come to find out, the U.S. Secret Service cut off major transport routes during the visit of a high-level political figure. I decided to continue north toward the border on my own, when I came across a camp leader who had other plans for me.

What I learned from being held hostage in the desert, is that it's important to know who you are and to understand how people perceive you. Your age, race, gender, nationality, and social status will shape people's perceptions of you and your intentions toward them. Understanding who you are and being able to clearly communicate your mission will help you stay the course. Sometimes you have to adjust your plans based on others' bad intentions.

Here's what happened.

Turning 21 in the Desert

I turned 21 in the middle of nowhere, drinking a strange cocktail with people I didn't know. They were Peace Corps volunteers from across the Sahara Desert who came to meet me, to help with the refugee project. I needed their help because it was my first visit to the border. They helped me prepare for a future trip with the human rights group. We would be conducting a census to count thousands of refugees forcibly evicted from their land.

The refugees were black Moors from Mauritania enslaved by the ruling white Arab class until slavery was outlawed in 1980. (Think about that again. In Mauritania, slavery was only outlawed in 1980. Prior to that, the white Arab ruling class enslaved darker-skinned people.) I knew about the refugees from the office of the United Nations High Commissioner for Refugees (UNHCR) in Dakar. They referred me to this organization because they were trying to negotiate the refugees' return. Although the government of Mauritania didn't want them, the human rights group held out hope that smaller groups of refugees could go back in phases over time.

In order to travel with the human rights group, I needed local contacts. As a young American woman, the Peace Corps gave me a built-in network of people to track my movement across remote parts of the desert. Over drinks in dim candlelight, the volunteers told me tales of local folklore. Cultural norms and hang-ups about sexual relationships was a favorite topic.

"Legend has it, the most alluring women in the desert are actually possessed by demons," one guy said. *"The men are afraid of attractive women disguised as evil spirits. They believe seductive women will make them demon possessed."*

We laughed as we drank our warm cocktails; it's hard to find ice in the desert, but easy to find comradery among fellow travelers. The conversation also turned to practical matters about my upcoming trip. One volunteer asked,

"Who will you be traveling with when you come next time?"
"I'll be with a human rights group."
"Are they planning to use local transportation?"
"Probably; it's a rather low budget operation," I said.
"It's better for you to have your own transportation," he said. *"You can use my driver. He can also translate for you."*
"Great idea; thanks so much," I replied.

As the sun went down, nomadic music started to play at the bar. We fell silent as the sun descended over the desert, casting shadows like waves of rose across an endless landscape of sand.

When I went to bed that night, I felt like everything was settled. The next time I came up to the desert, I would have a network of support in case anything went wrong. (More about this in a later chapter.) The Peace Corps volunteers would be my backup in case I ran into trouble.

Or so I thought.

From the capital city of Dakar, there is one road north. It goes through Thies, a transit town with one road in and out of town. That is where I was supposed to meet up with Amadou, the head of the group who was familiar with the refugee camps.

We had a plan that included a map of all the camps and a day-by-day itinerary that would give us enough time to count the number of refugees for the census. We needed to know who wanted to return from each camp location. We planned to meet in Thies. From there, we would take a local taxi, known as a "Tap-Tap" because people tapped the outside to get on board and tapped the inside to request a stop.

I sat in Thies for a long time waiting for Amadou, but he did not come. It was getting late. The sun was setting, and I didn't want to be traveling up to the desert at dark. I had to make a choice: return to Dakar and abandon the trip, or push north-ward on my own, following the plan until I met him up north. What I didn't know was that First Lady Hillary Clinton was in Thies that day, visiting a women's program. I also didn't know that the U.S. Secret Service closed the road, cutting Amadou off from where he was supposed to meet me.

I had to think quick, to salvage the plan.

I decided to take the Tap-Tap north on my own. It was a fateful decision. As I looked out across the vast desert, I felt confident everything would work out. Surely, Amadou would be at the first refugee camp on the list, waiting for me.

Days later, I found myself staring at iron weapons hanging on the wall of a thatched hut alongside pictures of a military commander dressed for battle. The weapons and pictures belonged to a refugee camp leader—who was in charge of the second camp on my list. He was listening to me intently as I tried to talk with him about conducting a census of the population.

As the man stared at me, smiling strangely, my "local partner," Amadou, came to mind. *Where could he be?* I wondered.

Doesn't everyone know that when things go wrong, it's important to stick to the plan? It began to occur to me that I was out on a limb.

When I didn't find Amadou in the first camp on our list, I contacted the Peace Corps volunteers, accepting their offer to use their local driver. But the volunteers wanted to come along to help the refugees. However, they didn't know anything about refugees and how important it was to have an accurate census to plan for their return home. Having the volunteers in conversations with the camp leaders, however well-meaning they were, was a distraction from my mission.

I decided that I would talk to the next camp leader on my own. But this, the second camp, was more isolated. It was hours from any villages, and the driver who brought me there did not want to stay all day.

I was not thinking. I made the mistake of telling the driver to leave me behind and come back for me in a few hours. I thought I would be fine, since I spoke French and some Pular, a local language. I thought I could get by on my own.

I wasn't counting on other agendas coming into play.

The camp leader was now leering at me. I didn't think about how I would be perceived as a single, young, white woman showing up at the camp leader's hut by myself. When I presented myself at the thatched door and asked to speak with him in his tent, he looked amused. I started to talk about the census and the human rights organization that wanted to include his camp in the population data. He wanted to talk about other things.

"What good is a census when we have a cholera outbreak?" he asked me. I explained my interest in helping these remote villages. He wasn't listening.

"The water is no good, and there's not enough of it."

"The program they have in mind will be able to help...." I tried to explain.

"My wife has died, leaving me with two small children." He looked at me slyly.

"I need another wife."

That went by me, and I continued to emphasize that the census would help produce evidence of their need for food and water so humanitarian agencies can help them. Having an accurate number of the people who want to return to Mauritania would provide a real solution so people could return and farm the land for themselves.

The atmosphere in the hut changed.

"Who are you, a young woman speaking to me like this, traveling through the desert without a father or brother to defend your honor?"

Now I was taken aback. I felt queasy in my stomach. I remembered that I was in a traditional Muslim society. I was in the middle of nowhere, a foreigner in a foreign land.

"It is our custom to take women like you as wives," he said. I was searching for something to say to counter him. ("That's flattering, but....")

"You will be my new wife," he proclaimed.

A light went off in my mind. In his eyes, I was the vulnerable one. He saw me as a young woman. How could I possibly help him?

Courage came from somewhere inside.

"No, I am not here on my own," I replied, keeping my voice as steady as I could.

"I am here with a human rights organization. My co-workers are asking the same questions in other camps."

But he persisted. *"You look alone to me. I am a serious man. See, I have commanded forces in a war."* He pointed out the pictures of him in military uniform along the wall, alongside the iron weapons.

"I can take you to be my wife."

I knew I was in trouble. My thoughts started to scramble—but then I remembered the folklore about women possessed by demons and that men are afraid to have sex with them.

With a cool voice, I said, *"You are right. I am not a good woman. That is why I am here alone."*

He looked at me inquisitively.

I began to curse in the Pular language, cursing my mother and my womb, the earth and all created things.

His eyes opened wide.

"I am a bad woman," I said, louder, hoping this might hold him back from attacking me.

He seemed a little hesitant, but then he called another man into the hut. *"Send a message down to the next village and tell this woman's driver not to come back for her. Tell him she wants to stay longer 'for the census.'"*

What had I done, coming here alone, thinking my support team had my back no matter what?

I began to foam at the mouth and pull out my hair, trying to make him think I was demon possessed. I didn't want him to come close or reach for one of the weapons on the wall. I wanted to create distance. I put up the charade long enough for him to wonder,

Is she really mad?

The charade seemed to go on forever, with me cursing and raving—all the while keeping him at a distance when he seemed to want to move in on me.

Eventually, as the sun was coming down, I heard a truck outside. My driver had come for me—finally.

"Stay here," the camp leader ordered as he went outside to check on the vehicle.

I dashed out of his tent and ran for the truck.

The camp leader was negotiating for the driver to leave me. *"I will give you goats in exchange for the woman,"* he offered.

There were no animals in the camp. They, too, had died.

"No," I insisted. *"I am leaving. Immediately,"* I added, signaling the driver. I turned to the camp leader and told him, in his language, *"I am not for sale."*

I got in and instructed the driver to take me to the next Peace Corps village.

I would sleep for the next three days, exhausted from the intensity of being under threat. From this experience, I realized that no matter what my intentions were, my identity would shape people's perception of me. I may see myself as an able-bodied helper with a sharp mind, but that is not how everyone else perceives me. **My age, race, and gender identity meant something to the people I was trying to help. Despite my best efforts, it got in the way of what I was trying to achieve.**

Likewise, who you are and what you look like—your nationality and social status—will be surmised by people wherever you go. Your ability to explain who you are and your motives, and to think quick under pressure, just might save your life.

The camp leader saw me as a young, idealistic, and single white female. He wanted other things from me. He could have hurt me and kept me from accomplishing my mission. But I didn't let his advances wear me down.

To finish the story of my harrowing experience: I persevered, moving on to the third camp after resting. There, I found Amadou at last.

"Why didn't you go to the other camps first?" I asked.

He looked at me, wide-eyed, and said,

"Those people are crazy. This camp is the best one."

After another month, we completed the census. The human rights group continued to advocate for the return of refugees expelled from their homes. I went back to Boston, entering my senior year of college. That same year, democratic elections in Mauritania ushered in a new government, allowing half of the refugees—about 30,000 people—to return home in 2008. The census we completed enabled the return to be organized so people could reclaim their land.

Here's another important moral to this story. Despite the obstacles you face, your work can achieve a bigger picture of changing people's lives for the better. When you persevere, you can achieve a greater good than any difficulty you might face. You can help thousands of people have a chance to go home and start over.

When you are working in a cross-cultural environment, know who you are and why you are there. You have to understand how people perceive you and know when they become a threat. By learning how to take calculated risks, you can stay alive.

What a story you will tell when one day, you also face down giants along your path.

Nearly Killed

Aid workers face numerous threats to their physical safety. These threats can come from armed groups or from the very people they are trying to help. There are also risks to your safety in every environment. One of the greatest threats to aid worker safety is traffic accidents.

Given the unregulated roads that lead to reckless driving, hundreds of aid workers a year die in traffic accidents. I had one such near-death experience while on assignment in South Africa.

I learned to drive a manual stick-shift in Johannesburg which was a feat in and of itself. It was a hilly city, and there were many unwritten rules of the road. One of them is that you never completely stop at a stop sign; otherwise, you might get car jacked.

Car hijackings are common in South Africa. When drivers stop long enough at a stop sign, thieves are oftentimes standing by to steal the car. This often happens forcibly, at gunpoint. Everyone told me: to save your life, do not stop. Pause at the stop sign or red light and then roll right on through. Johannesburg is a high-altitude city with rolling hills, which makes not stopping hard because you don't want to roll the car downhill.

One day, when I actually did make a full stop on the way to work, I was hit by a drunk driver going 180 kilometers—that's **110 miles per hour.** Even though I looked both ways, I didn't see him coming. After the driver hit me, he ran his car into the house next door. Then, he came up to me, reeking of alcohol.

"Why did you hit me, man?" he asked me with arms flailing. His grand gestures were confusing to me. The impact was so great, I wasn't sure if I could get out of the car. The vehicle crushed around me like an accordion. Taking stock of my limbs, I was glad to see they were all still attached to my body.

Once I got out of the car, I was barely able to stand. Even though an ambulance came to the scene, I didn't go to the hospital at first. I wasn't bleeding, and I couldn't see any injuries. But, by the time a colleague took me home, I could no longer remember my name or address. I asked a neighbor to take me to the hospital.

There I was in the emergency room of the hospital, and I could not remember my own name. They asked me several times for my personal identifying information. I tried really hard to remember who I was, but nothing came to me. I tried to remember my address, but I couldn't remember where I lived.

I stared at the registration form on the hospital desk and told the nurse, *"I can't remember anything."*

Everything seemed distant, except for the overhead lights shining in my eyes.

She asked me again, *"What is your name?"*

"I don't know," I said. *"I just don't know."* I was hit so hard; I didn't know what happened.

"How long ago was the accident?" she asked.

"Minutes ago," I responded. *"Less than an hour."*

I wanted to wipe a strand of hair that had strayed across one eye but couldn't seem to make my hands do what I wanted.

The nurse called for a wheelchair and signaled for help.

"Take her back immediately," she said to the orderly, then turned to me again. *"Who is this with you,"* she asked and, perhaps to help me out, pointed to the older gentleman sitting in the waiting room.

"My neighbor," I acknowledged. *"He brought me to the hospital."*

"Is he family? Can he make decisions about your care?"

"No. I don't have any family in this country," I said.

She hesitated, then took a deep breath. *"We are afraid you might be paralyzed or are suffering severe nerve damage. Be very still. Try not to move at all. We are taking you back."*

Emergency room nurses surrounded me and wheeled me to the back room. There were about eight of them, all men, speaking different languages. Some Afrikaans, some Zulu, some Xhosa. Very carefully, they lifted and placed me on an operating table.

Then, one of the nurses said, in English, "*We are going to strap your arms and legs down so you can't move. We need to make sure you're not paralyzed.*"

His words terrified me. "*Can I call someone first?*"

I should have someone here with me, I thought. *But who?*

I switched my phone on and tried to access the most recent numbers I had dialed.

I remembered my friend, Sarita. She would come if she knew where I was. But I had no idea where I was. What would I tell her?

The phone went dead before I could dial out.

I began to cry. I was all alone.

To make things worse, the male nurses took out several large pairs of scissors and began cutting off my clothes.

I cried some more as the men stripped me down. I closed my eyes to pray. I prayed that I was not paralyzed. Thankfully, x-rays showed that while my skeletal frame had shifted, causing a painful disconnect between my bones and muscle tissue that would require physical therapy, I was not paralyzed.

Eventually, I recovered at the home of a doctor who offered to take care of me. He mostly let me sleep and rest. I didn't want to see anyone while I was healing. My entire body was bruised, turning shades of black, purple, and green until the internal bleeding stopped.

For a while, I had dreams about the accident every day. In my dreams, I died as a result of my injuries. Realizing that I had been through a traumatic incident, I sought counseling to manage my recurring fears. The bad dreams stopped, my bruising healed, and I also received physical therapy to help my body recover from the shock. To this day, I cannot go on amusement rides, like roller coasters, that remind me of being jostled by the accident. I was lucky to come out of that one alive.

Health Risks

In addition to these critical incidents, living overseas exposes you to health risks. In southern Afghanistan, the sewer system had long been damaged by the war. Windstorms that carried dust also carried fecal matter because people would openly defecate in the street.

Most of the livestock died as a result of water shortages from the drought. When our cook managed to find meat in the market, we assumed the animals were transported overland on dusty roads from Pakistan. Becoming ill immediately after eating was a frequent occurrence. In order to adjust, I tried to eat less meat and ensure the vegetables were adequately washed.

In other assignments, I contracted mosquito and water-borne diseases including malaria and giardia, both of which took long recoveries. As a precaution from mosquitos, I now treat my clothes with permethrin to repel insects, and I make sure to wear longer garments in tropical climates. To manage water-related illnesses, I find out whether the hotel I'm staying at has a filtration system. Many do not, so I avoid opening my mouth in the shower and brushing my teeth with local water. I've learned the hard way not to swim in local pools or watering holes, even when I'm terribly hot and would love to dive in. Some of my worst illnesses have come from such fun times.

I also have a travel doctor on speed dial who can update my vaccinations and prescribe emergency medicine for specific locations, so I have medications on hand when needed. The travel doctor, who specializes in tropical infectious diseases, also educates me about a variety of symptoms, so I know what medication to take if I get sick in places where there is no doctor.

If you return home from an assignment and are sick, it is important that you see a doctor with expertise in international health. Many doctors in the U.S. are not trained to recognize these illnesses from other countries, and some common laboratory tests do not detect certain conditions. You have to remain vigilant to stay healthy in the field, and you need the right doctor to treat you when you do get sick.

Sometimes, even the best conditions can lead to life-threatening illnesses. For example, when I lived in West Africa, I slept on the floor because mattresses were a luxury item. I used a mosquito net which hung from the ceiling to prevent bites at night, but one morning, I woke up with a strange mark on my face. Thinking that it was a pimple, I squeezed the mark. Within minutes, my entire face swelled up like a balloon. I called a friend for advice, and she gave me the number of a specialist. When I got to his office, he inspected the mark. I had been bitten by a fatally poisonous spider, and when I squeezed the mark, poison spread over my face. If the poison spread from my face to my earlobe, it could have entered my brain and killed me. The doctor gave me injections every hour, monitoring me for twenty-four hours to make sure I did not die. Thankfully, the injections worked, and the swelling went down.

Here's the lesson in all this. **Do not take your health for granted. When you are sick, you are not able to help anyone.**

Take care of yourself first. Be on the watch for threats to your own well-being.

Managing Risk

By now you may be thinking that I was really unlucky to have these experiences. But that's not the point. Even if you stay home and help people close by, you need to look out for yourself.

If you do end up working in conflict and disaster zones, you will be exposed to risk. In some ways, I was lucky. I got out of every situation alive, with some measure of dignity and a good dose of reality and knowledge.

A few friends of mine have not been so lucky. Some of my colleagues have been raped, held hostage for months on end, and killed. I have also helped organizations whose staff were held hostage in remote areas. I will never forget sitting down with the leader of a large organization, who, despite his many contacts with the embassy and the military, was unable to locate a young member of the staff who was taken by an armed group. I was in the uncomfortable position of asking if the risk of expanding operations to this area was worth losing their staff. Every decision you make about where to help has trade-offs.

How can you tell whether the place you're going to is safe or not? **Do your research.** Study security incidents and armed groups in the area. Cultivate local contacts who can warn you about dangerous areas. The Aid Worker Security database tracks incidents involving violence against aid workers. Since the project started tracking reported incidents in 2005, nearly

5,000 aid workers have been wounded, killed, or kidnapped.[15] The database tracks information by country, so you can see where aid workers are being targeted. This and other sources of information, such as maps on Relief Web, an online portal managed by the United Nations, can help you understand the risks you will face in specific countries.

Be Prepared

Here's the main point of these stories: you need to be prepared. Here are a few tips to help you as you prepare for any assignment:

Understand your racial, gender, and cultural identity, and understand the cultural and societal norms where you are working. Maintain awareness of perceptions and attitudes toward foreigners and be alert.

Do not become isolated from your colleagues. Work in pairs or teams. Make sure that someone is aware of your travel plans and movements.

Be in good physical health before you go. Get your vaccinations, and take emergency medication with you in advance for diarrhea and stomach pain. Stay hydrated with clean water. Take your health seriously.

Practice good mental health. Exercise on a regular basis. Practice yoga, mindfulness, prayer, or breathing techniques to

---

[15]For more information, see the Aid Worker Security database managed by Humanitarian Outcomes; https://aidworkersecurity.org/incidents/report/victims

stay calm in stressful situations. Be mindful of a happy place or memory to focus on when you are in a difficult place.

Work for organizations that are prepared with a good security plan that can get you out of a hot zone fast when necessary. Ask the organization for its security plan, review it, and make sure they have good risk insurance.

Research risks where you are going, including security incident maps so you can identify what type of danger is occurring in areas where you will operate. If you are going to a conflict zone, be aware of armed groups operating in the area.

Get training on hostile environments. Ask your organization what type of training is available. Look for online training that is specific to your location.

Debrief after each mission. This can be as simple as out-processing with colleagues or seeing a professional counselor to discuss traumatic events.

Keep up your professional network and have a close circle of friends. Network with other relief workers online and ask questions about local conditions where you are going.

Talk with your friends and family about your experience. Don't lose contact with people. Maintain your personal connections.

Take Care of Yourself—You Are Needed

Helping people is a great privilege. Walking alongside those who are suffering is rewarding when you see your work having a measurable impact on people's lives.

However, caring for humanity also has its risks. Hazards of the trade include illness, injury, mental trauma, and risk of death. When bad things happen, it is not a result of your individual choices. Rather, in any complex emergency, you are in a situation well beyond your control. When public order breaks down, you are also at-risk of random attacks. Armed groups in a conflict zone may see you as simply being in their way. Even if you follow all the rules, you could be at the wrong place at the wrong time.

The first step to coping with these risks begins with understanding yourself and the environment around you.

Knowing what danger lies ahead, being prepared for specific country conditions, remaining in coordination with your colleagues on the ground and complying with security rules—all these efforts can save your life.

Putting your security first might also mean saying no to opportunities that are too risky. For example, I was offered a position in Rwanda, in a volatile region near the border of the Democratic Republic of the Congo (DRC). The organization wanted me to live in the office, where they stored all their cash to implement projects. I would be the only person living and working in the house—alone. In the event of an evacuation, there was only one road out of the area to the capital city, and rebels frequently held up cars on the route.

I declined the offer based on security concerns and took another assignment.

You may be eager to start out, or you may be ready to try something new. Regardless of how you choose to help others, be mindful of the risks involved. You are a precious resource. Ensuring your own health and safety is critical to your capacity to help others. And besides that, *you want to live a good, long life—don't you?*

Later on, we will also talk about the importance of creating a support network. This is especially critical when you see bad things happening and you cannot stop the violence or change conditions right away. Sometimes, you will have to take a different approach.

On really hard days, you will have to rely on your core belief in humanity and faith that a better world is possible.

You will need to lean on your colleagues and trusted friends. One day you may choose to work toward even bigger changes. I have found that one of the toughest problems to overcome in the field is violence against women and girls. The next chapter explores why this violence is a global crisis of epidemic proportions.

6

ME TOO: A GLOBAL CRISIS

Of all the problems I've worked to address, sexual violence has confounded me the most. **Globally, 1 in 3 women will experience sexual violence in her lifetime.** This is a world-wide phenomenon. The World Health Organization (WHO) has collected global prevalence data indicating that women and girls are more likely to suffer violence at the hands of a family member or an intimate partner than a stranger or member of an armed group.[16]

This chapter is about understanding why sexual violence is taking place so you can help end the cycle of violence. This problem affects both men and women in every country and people of all socio-economic backgrounds.[17] It is not contained to one place or ethnic group.

Sexual violence affects men and women everywhere. It is, in fact, a global crisis.

Experts will tell you that gender-based violence is rooted in gender bias and cultural norms that prefer men to women, denying females equal rights and opportunities. These biases are manifested in different forms of discrimination and harmful practices. Many countries still have discriminatory laws and

---

[16]For more information, see the World Health Organization (WHO) report, Global and regional estimates of violence against women, 2013.
[17]For more information, see World Bank and WHO research on the prevalence of violence against women and girls worldwide.

policies that deny women basic human rights and economic advancement compared to men.

Violence against women is a global phenomenon—it affects women everywhere, not only in developing countries but also in industrialized ones. It is especially prevalent in humanitarian crisis settings, where a breakdown in social order leads to increased vulnerability for women and children.

Refugees and displaced women are especially vulnerable to sexual violence as they flee to safety. The definition of a refugee **is a person with a well-founded fear of persecution on account of one of five factors: their race, religion, political opinion, nationality, or membership of a particular social group.** The legal definition of "a particular social group" has been significantly disputed in immigration courts to determine whether a person's gender makes them part of a vulnerable social group. However, it is clear to me that an individual can be targeted for violence on account of one's gender preference.

I have seen men and women suffer sexual violence. I, too, have my own personal journey of experiencing this crisis. By sharing my story, I want to help you recognize the root cause of this problem and help you to protect those around you.

My Story

I know about the devastating impact of sexual violence on a woman's life because I experienced it as a child. Growing up in suburban America as a blonde-haired, blue-eyed girl, you might assume that I have always lived a privileged life. But this is not the case. When I was young, my father left our family. I grew up with my brother and a single mom who worked hard to make ends meet. Living on one income, our family was eligible for social benefits like food stamps and free lunches at school.

Because I lived this way, I can better identify with people who are in need. I can identify with people who are afraid because I have also been afraid. This ability to recognize people in need is one of the greatest assets I bring to humanitarian work.

Early in my life, I realized that being female was going to bring unique challenges. As a young girl, I didn't know what it meant to be vulnerable. I wanted to be a superhero like Princess Leia in Star Wars, who defended Luke Skywalker from his archenemies. I also wanted to be like Miss Piggy from the Muppets Show, who had a big, bold personality that shined. Like these characters, I saw myself as equally capable as my male peers.

I didn't know it at the time, but I was vulnerable. I learned the hard way that I needed to protect myself. An early experience of childhood abuse opened my eyes to the problem of sexual violence **in America, where 1 out of 6 women are violated in their lifetime.** Some people dispute these numbers, saying they are inflated.

You may be wondering: *how could so many women be violated?* I do not dispute the numbers. I have seen the evidence in my work, and I know from personal experience. The strong prey upon the weak. Men use physical force to exert control and express anger. Sex can be used as a weapon of fear, submission, and even war.

In every neighborhood, there are women and girls, and boys and men, who will experience sexual violence. Perhaps you have experienced this kind of violence, either personally or through a friend. You are not alone, and help is available to you.[18]

Telling My Mother

"No one should touch you that way, ever. Do you hear me?" my mom said, exasperated, as we left a family event. Then she repeated, *"No one should touch you in a way you do not like."*

My cousin had just thrown a few punches at me. I had no idea why she was hitting me, but she wouldn't stop. So, I did what eight-year-olds do; I went to get my mom.

As we were pulling out of the driveway, I was no longer thinking about my cousin. I was thinking about what my mom just said. *"No one should touch you in a way you do not like, ever."*

I felt sick to my stomach. Something was wrong, very wrong. Someone was touching me in an even worse way, and I needed to tell her.

When Mom came to tuck me into bed that night, I told her who was touching me and how sick it was making me. I was getting sick over it every night.

Easter Sunday

Hours earlier, the day had started beautifully. I woke up and got dressed in a translucent purple dress. It was Easter

---

[18]For U.S. survivors of sexual assault, there are phone and online hotlines available at the Rape, Abuse and Incest National Network (RAINN) website www.rainn.org and a National Domestic Violence Hotline at www.thehelpline.org. For international survivors, see the UN Women Global Knowledge Platform to End Violence Against Women to find out about prevention efforts and service providers by country, https://evaw.unwomen.org/en

Sunday—and also my First Communion in the Catholic Church. When I walked down the grassy aisle to receive communion at the sunrise service, I offered a child-like prayer,

God, if you are real, show me a sign. Help me.

The sign came after I spoke up and told my mother, and it came in the form of a woman who was brave and strong enough to protect her daughter. A few days later, I was at the police station, explaining what had happened to me.

Today, all these years later, I can still recall the feeling of being afraid. The situation was beyond my ability to control. When I see that look of fear in someone's eyes, I recognize it intimately. I want to protect that person, but I also want to help those affected regain control over their lives.

Ultimately, the cycle of violence ends when perpetrators are held accountable for their actions. Victims can be a powerful witness for preventing future abuse. As survivors tell their story, they take control over their lives. They are not defeated by what happened to them or by their circumstances. They are survivors, and **survivors change the world.**

It's <u>NOT</u> about Sex

The first thing you need to understand is that **sexual violence is not about sexual acts. It is fundamentally about power.** It is about one person or group of persons overpowering another. This struggle for dominance can take many forms of abuse, including domestic violence, child abuse, rape, intimate partner violence, forced marriage, and psychological harm. These forms of harm that are based on one's gender are also known as Gender Based Violence (GBV).

Although violence against women is a world-wide phenomenon, there is a greater likelihood that women will experience violence by someone they know than by a stranger. However, during a conflict or a disaster, women and girls become more vulnerable to attacks perpetrated by armed groups and criminal gangs, in addition to partners and family members. While men and boys also experience sexual violence, including rape, slavery, and forced sterilization, this occurs on a more limited basis.

Gender Dynamics in Emergencies

One reason behind the surge in violence in emergency settings is that during a crisis, men and women experience significant changes in their social status. In a crisis, men, who are the head of household and provider for their families, often experience significant loss such as unemployment and losing their homes or financial status. The resulting frustration often fuels physical, psychological, and substance abuse with compounding effects.

When families become displaced, they undergo significant stress from losing their homes and sense of place. Men react to these conditions differently than women. Some men join armed groups to protect their communities or engage in criminal activity, including purchasing supplies for their families on the black market. Many men migrate in search of work to send money home. Others abuse alcohol and drugs, inducing violent behavior.

Like men, women also experience significant changes when a crisis occurs. In conflict zones, many women lose their male relatives to fighting, becoming widows and single heads of the household for the first time. Women and children unaccompanied by male relatives become vulnerable to predators.

Displaced women also lose their sense of place in society, not knowing how to relate to the people around them. Refugee camps are formed out of chaos after families have already been separated. Imagine how scary it is for women in traditional societies, like Syria and Iraq, who are expected to work at home and care for their families, to be in a refugee camp, an unfamiliar place surrounded by people they do not know.[19]

These gender dynamics are repeated in humanitarian crises throughout the world. On average, men and women each comprise 50 percent of the population. This balance is turned upside down in refugee contexts, where women and children can make up to 80 percent of the population, as men often leave the area to find work or join armed groups.

In many places where women and children are living without male relatives, they are exploited by armed groups, criminal gangs, and smugglers. Children are particularly vulnerable to being recruited as child soldiers, as sex slaves, and for forced labor or human trafficking from places such as refugee camps, orphanages, and schools. Each year, the United Nations releases a report listing which armed groups are recruiting child soldiers in order to hold governments accountable for reducing this harmful practice.[20] This is why some people within the humanitarian sector focus on the protection of vulnerable groups. Protection involves identifying people at-risk of being

---

[19]For more information about the impact of war on Syrian women, see my paper on *Syrian Women in Crisis: Obstacles and Opportunities*, Georgetown University Occasional Paper Series on Women's Economic Participation in Conflict-Affected and Fragile Settings, January 2016.

[20]The Secretary General of the United Nations submits an annual report to the UN Security Council on the Situation of Children and Armed Conflict (CAAC). These reports are available at https://childrenandarmedconflict.un.org/

exploited and then developing ways to keep them safe within their community.

Mrs. Chan—The Philippines

When a refugee family becomes separated by war, it can take years to bring them back together. I have worked to reunite refugee families, and it's a messy business. After years of separation, as husbands and wives live apart and children no longer live with their parents, it's hard to put families back together again.

I dealt with family reunification cases for Vietnamese refugees in the Philippines when I worked in a legal aid office in Manila, the capital. Thousands of refugees were living there, decades after the war ended. We saw all kinds of broken families, families that had been torn apart and families that were breaking under the pressure of living as foreigners without the right to work. The office helped many of these refugees to eventually resettle in the United States.

Each day, I worked through a translator to recreate the life history of each refugee, spending up to three hours with each person, listening to how they were persecuted in Vietnam. When I needed a break from the intensity of the stories, I went up to the roof, where a small Filipino church gathered and children played. After joining the children in whatever game they were playing that day, I would go back down to the office and start working with another client.

Although we operated as a legal aid office, it often felt like a family crisis center.

One afternoon, Mrs. Chan came running into the office crying, asking for the office director. When she saw him, she sobbed. Her husband was drunk again. He was beating her severely.

"Tell him to stop," she exclaimed. *"Tell him to stop!"*

The office director listened to Mrs. Chan intently, nodding his head continuously. Afterward, we went into a closed-door meeting to discuss the situation.

"What are you going to do?" I asked him. "You know all the men respect you. They will listen to whatever you say."

"Yes," he said, "but Mr. Chan is my elder. In our culture, I cannot confront him."

"What good is it," I asked, "to document their persecution while Mrs. Chan is afraid for her life? This is not a time for saving face. Go talk to him!" I exclaimed.

"But Sarah, you don't understand," he continued. "Domestic violence is prevalent among the refugee families...and in our culture."

"Then talk to *all the men*," I said. "You don't have to confront Mr. Chan directly. Tell *all of them* they should stop beating their wives."

I had seen the men get drunk day after day, the listless look on their faces from being repeatedly turned down for work because they lacked identity documents. Being refugees in a country not their own, they lost hope for a better future. They needed to be resettled in another country in order to have the right to work and continue to educate their children.

"If you need to save face, then blame the talk on me," I said. "Tell them I don't want to see women beat up. Tell them that in America, domestic violence is a crime that will land them in jail. They better stop now."

The director called a meeting with all the men. I went along, standing there with my hands on my hips and a stern look on my face. There was no translation from Vietnamese to English, so I didn't understand what he was saying to them. Near the end, I asked, "Did you tell them that domestic violence is against the law in the United States?"

He shook his head and gave me a stern look. I wanted to make sure the men understood my point. "Make sure you tell them that if they hit their wives in the United States, it is illegal."

Then, he looked downward and closed with a few sad words. In Vietnamese culture, women do not tell men what to do—but I had to do my part. Speaking up for Mrs. Chan allowed us to speak up for *all the women* in her community.

I couldn't let Mrs. Chan's plea go unaddressed. I had seen the devastating impact of domestic violence before. I knew that it could get far worse for Mrs. Chan and other women like her if the men continued with the beatings.

I had seen it for myself—in South Africa.

Women's Ward, South Africa

Living in Johannesburg, I was confronted with gruesome stories of sexual violence on a daily basis. The press competed with one another for the most grotesque story of the day. Each morning, the graphic headlines were affixed to telephone poles at every street corner so that drivers passing by would be shocked and buy more papers. When I first saw the headlines, I, too, was shocked.

"Infant of two months gang raped by four men"
"Child disfigured, torn apart by sex"

As the headlines grew worse, I began to wonder—were the stories true? I asked local doctors if people were really raping infants. It seemed unfathomable to me. Yes, they told me. There is no limit to how small the child is—infant rape cases come into the hospital every day. What could be behind this, I wondered?

There was a popular belief among men that raping a child gave them immunity from being infected by the HIV virus that causes AIDS. Infected men were trying to "cure" themselves this way, stealing children and permanently disfiguring their reproductive organs.

"You should see what they do to the women. It is even worse," the doctors said. The doctors invited me to join them for morning rounds at the hospital in Soweto, the biggest township in Johannesburg. I joined them one Saturday morning.

Soweto Hospital

The hospital floors of Soweto hospital were covered in blood. Realizing the risk of infection, I dressed in surgical scrubs before making rounds. Although I only intended to observe the rounds, I soon found myself alone in the women's ward.

I stood dumbfounded as I tried not to stare at the women, who were mutilated in the most intimate places. A resident physician from Cuba came alongside me, motioning me to the bedside of a woman who was losing a breast. It was nearly cut off by a large knife wound. The resident asked for my help.

"Can you hold her breast for me?" he asked.

"Uh, I'm not qualified to work on patients," I said.

"We need to sew her up or else she's going to lose this breast. Do you see anyone else around here who's available?" he implored.

There were women everywhere groaning in pain—but no other doctors or nurses. There was no one else to help. Not one woman was on an intravenous (IV) drip or pain medication.

As the resident prepared a large needle to sew the breast back on, I wanted to apologize to the woman for not giving her any pain medication, but she was barely lucid. I carefully held her breast, hoping we could save it from falling off completely. When the resident stitched her breast back on, the woman passed out.

"Better that she sleeps now," he said, urging me on to the next patient. We continued down the row, but all I could think about was that one woman's breast.

"Who did that to her?" I wondered out loud.

The resident replied, "Probably someone she knows," and motioned me onward.

In fact, intimate partner violence (IPV) affects significant numbers of women throughout the African continent. Prevalence studies by the World Health Organization (WHO) indicate that nearly half of all African women and girls will experience violence from a partner in her lifetime.[21]

---

[21]See World Health Organization (WHO), Global and regional data on violence against women, 2013.

Being in the hospital that day made me realize that we need to provide better health care for women affected by violence. It also made me realize this:

Sexual violence is like an epidemic. To find a cure, the disease needs to be cut off at its source, attacking the inequalities and belief systems that devalue women.

War Crimes

Sexual violence is not restricted to inter-personal violence between two people. During times of war, sexual violence is used on a large scale to intimidate and control entire groups. When armed groups use rape as a weapon of war, this is called Conflict Related Sexual Violence (CRSV).

In the 1990s, rape was used as a form of ethnic cleansing in Bosnia-Herzegovina and the Rwanda genocide. Prior to this, the international community understood rape as an inevitable consequence of war.[22] Then, between 1992 and 1994, as many as 20,000 Bosnian women were brutally enslaved, raped, and tortured by Serbian and Bosnian military forces in the former Yugoslavia. In 1996, the International Criminal Tribunal for the Former Yugoslavia (ICTY) prosecuted police and military officers for rape as a war crime and as a crime against humanity, including officers who ordered soldiers to rape under their command.

During the same period, the International Criminal Tribunal for Rwanda (ICTR) was established to prosecute those responsible for the genocide that systematically killed 800,000 ethnic Tutsi in merely one hundred days between April and July 1994. During

---

[22]Nahapetian, Kate. Selective Justice: Prosecuting Rape in the International Criminal Tribunals for the Former Yugoslavia and Rwanda. 14 Berkeley Women's L.J. 126 (1999).

the mass killings, Hutu military commanders gave orders for men to rape women with the express purpose of impregnating them and re-engineering the ethnicity of their children. It is estimated that "hundreds of thousands" of Rwandan women were raped, as evidenced by the many women who abandoned their offspring after giving birth.[23] As a result of what happened in Rwanda, the International Criminal Court (ICC) also determined that rape could be prosecuted as an act of genocide.

Today, the United Nations documents Conflict Related Sexual Violence (CRSV) in war zones, holding armed groups accountable for reported violations. Each year, the UN Secretary General reports how many people are affected by sexual violence in active conflicts. Even though many cases of CRSV still go unreported, we can track the number of people affected from Myanmar to the Congo.

Studying these patterns of violence helps us learn how to end the cycle of violence, but more needs to be done to prevent sexual violence. Significant efforts are underway to fight against impunity, to hold armed groups accountable by establishing codes of conduct for military forces and enforcing a military code of justice. However, many countries are hampered by malfunctioning judicial systems and a weak rule of law, which allows perpetrators to go free.

Marital Rape

Even in peaceful societies, insufficient legal standards lead to gaps in accountability for the protection of women and

---

[23]McKinley, James. "Legacy of Rwanda Violence: The Thousands Born of Rape," *New York Times*, September 23, 1996.

children. In 2019, ten countries still considered marital rape and domestic violence to be private matters beyond the scope of legal recourse.[24] Some traditional societies even force young women to marry their rapist to preserve their "honor."

A landmark case in Morocco where a 15-year-old girl named Amina was forced to marry her rapist eventually led to changes in the law. The girl's father opposed the marriage but was powerless to stop it because a court mandated the marriage to preserve the girl's honor. After a few months of being married to her abuser, Amina committed suicide.

When Amina died in 2012, powerful women's groups from around the world put pressure on the Moroccan government to change the law. Now, young women like Amina are no longer forced to marry their abuser. That is the power of collective advocacy, of women coming together to stop the violence. Yet, it's shocking that cases like this still exist in the 21st Century.

You may be asking: ***How is it possible that women suffer this violence?*** When it comes to understanding conflict, there is considerable scholarship on the nature of war and conflict resolution. There are fewer answers for addressing the root cause of gender-based violence. However, let's explore a few schools of thought.

Patriarchy

When I try to understand the root cause of violence against women, I think back to a class I took in college on *Women and*

---

[24]According to the organization Equality Now, these countries are Ghana, India, Indonesia, Jordan, Lesotho, Nigeria, Oman, Singapore, Sri Lanka, and Tanzania.

World Politics. My professor, Dr. Sen, had a small stature, yet her peering eyes and expressive hands gave her an ominous presence. She commanded an audience, and she kept her students on their toes.

On the first day of class, she explained the concept of *patriarchy*. I had never heard this word before. Dr. Sen explained that it meant the world is designed by men, for men, and that all possessions and property, all legal entitlement—the very identity of children—was passed through men, not women. Even with her vivid explanation of the word, I had to look up the definition several times:

> **Patriarchy**: social organization marked by the supremacy of the father in the clan or family, the legal dependence of wives and children, and the reckoning of descent and inheritance in the male line *broadly*: control by men of a disproportionately large share of power
>
> Merriam-Webster Dictionary

The class studied patriarchy, focusing on societies where women had little to no power over decisions affecting their lives, such as where they lived, who they married, when they had children, and how much money they made or whether they could work.

The Taliban

Every student in Dr. Sen's class was given an independent research assignment to explain patriarchy in a particular place. I focused my project on the emergence of the Taliban in Afghanistan. The Taliban were stoning women to death for teaching girls to read and forcing women to cover up in a long, blue robe called a *burka*.

This was the worst form of patriarchy I could find. My research tracked how the Taliban used violence against women to take control of Afghanistan, instilling fear in the population town by town.

When I presented my research to the class, Dr. Sen explained that patriarchy is much subtler than this extreme case. She said that patriarchy is more nuanced than stoning women to death in a public square. It means that women take on the male name in the family they marry into; it means that property is passed down through the sons; in Biblical times it meant that the widow of a dead man became the property of his brother.

Dr. Sen continued to explain that in many societies today, as in the past, "*Women are a possession, a commodity to be owned, an item that can be sold, bartered, and traded in exchange for goods or services.*" I couldn't fathom what that could be like.

When Dr. Sen finished telling the class that I had not understood patriarchy, I told her, "*But here in America, women are free to own ourselves.*"

She did not agree. "*You think that is true,*" she said, "*but it is often not the case.*" I knew she was saying something profound, but I didn't fully understand her.

Today, I have a deeper understanding of Dr. Sen's message. Even in the United States, men play a dominant role in public and family life. Women are the dominant caregivers of children and older relatives. They still do the lion-share of household work. Yet, the decisions that men make have a significant impact on women's lives. This subtle form of control is often unrecognized and unacknowledged, leading to systematic inequalities.

For example, on average, women earn only 80 cents for every \$1 earned by a man for the same work. This wage gap leads women to work longer and harder to earn the same amount as men. Male politicians make decisions about women's health care, determining their access to birth control and childcare services. Women have had to fight for their rights, including the right to vote and own property, while men are freely given these opportunities. Men and women who don't conform to gender stereotypes also face discrimination and abuse. These gender dynamics reflect patriarchal values that have been passed down from generation to generation.

The Rise of Me Too

In late 2016, several major events led to the rebirth of the women's movement in the United States. The fiercely contested presidential election and the resurgence of conservative leadership that followed led to millions of women marching on Washington, D.C. and led to other marches of solidarity throughout the world, showing support for women's equality.

At the same time, cases of sexual assault in the sports and entertainment industry led to the rebirth of the *"Me Too"* movement whereby thousands of women shared their experience of being sexually assaulted on social media. The outpouring of numerous men and women expressing how they were violated brought a renewed awareness and openness to the extent of the problem.

Unequal power relations between men and women is a social construct that is reinforced by culture and belief systems. It is not always manifested in gross human rights violations such as rape and war crimes. Rather, gender inequality is about the small ways in which power dynamics within a society favor men over women, even within the family and at the household level.

The World Health Organization (WHO) recognizes acts of violence against women as a pattern of behavior that violates the rights of women and girls.[25] Thus, the way to end violence against women is to disrupt this pattern, preventing discrimination at every level, especially within the home and society at large.

How Can We Stop the Violence?

First, both men and women need to recognize that this discrimination occurs, then work to stand up to it together. Gender discrimination occurs in the home and the workplace, affecting the productivity of society. How male relatives view gender roles **within the family** is a critical factor in the likelihood of a woman being a success or being abused. Men can discriminate against women at home by exerting dominance and control, withholding finances and other forms of support from female relatives. **Within the workplace,** men help other men pursue economic and career opportunities at the expense of females who qualify for the same positions. If more men championed women's contributions at work, regardless of their personal interests, women would have a more equal chance of success.

Numerous times in my career, men offered to help me pursue a raise or job in exchange for sex, *including one senior United Nations official who threatened to withhold millions of dollars from "my refugee camps" if I refused to sleep with him.* Thankfully, I was able to tell him that my programs did not need the money.

---

[25]World Health Organization, Global and regional estimates of violence against women, 2013.

Young men rarely have this problem. This abuse of power is so widespread that the U.S. instituted sexual harassment laws to prevent systematic discrimination against women in the workplace. Yet, men can also be powerful champions for women, rooting for them and enabling their success by treating them equally alongside men.

Some men do not understand how gender discrimination manifests itself today. They deny the need for women's rights and for the rights of gender non-conformists within the lesbian, gay, bisexual, transgender, and queer (LGBTQ) community.

Yet, **men who take the time to listen to female friends, colleagues, and family members would know better.** Gender dynamics are passed down from generation to generation, and negative attitudes are manifested at home, at work, and throughout society in numerous ways.

Today, gender bias is often masked as sexism within institutions of work and governance, with sweeping implications for the well-being of women. Oftentimes, men and boys joke about sexism because it makes them uncomfortable to acknowledge they have the power to change these dynamics. It is hard for men to acknowledge how favoritism is passed through boys' clubs and male networks that tacitly or implicitly exclude women and other gender non-conformists.

In order for a man to pursue gender equality, he has to have the courage to stand out from the crowd. He has to acknowledge his power and exhibit a more inclusive masculinity that tolerates, accepts, and embraces gender equality. Few men take this uncomfortable position. Some men see the need for gender equality when they try to help younger generations of women, including their daughters, have equal opportunities in the workplace. This same concern for the future of their daughters and granddaughters can also guide their involvement in gender equality for all people.

"No man has a natural right to commit aggression on the natural rights of another, and this is all from which the law ought to restrain him."

Thomas Jefferson

Violence against women occurs because it is socially acceptable. Societies that devalue women in small ways become numb to the erosion of women's rights on a larger scale.

Thus, the best way to pursue gender equality is to have respect for men and women, giving them equal rights and legal benefits regardless of sex and sexual preference.

By virtue of their gender, men have a unique role to play in advancing the human rights and dignity of all people. Male authority figures, heads of households and heads of government, can support changes in gender norms by respecting women and holding one another accountable to higher standards of behavior. When men abuse women, they should face legal consequences.

As a society, we should respect the rights of women and girls, encouraging females to excel through work and education. Numerous studies have shown that as women's income and access to education increase, incidents of violence within the home decrease.[26] The economic and social advancement of women leads to healthy self-esteem, the benefits of which

---

[26]The international nonprofit Promundo and the U.S. Department of Justice (DOJ) have conducted numerous studies on the link between increases in women's income and decreases in the prevalence of domestic violence.

are passed on to children who have high expectations of themselves and a bright outlook for their future.

Nurturing a healthy self-esteem was an important aspect of my recovery from childhood abuse. When my case was brought to court, it resulted in a conviction that put a man in prison. The court also required me to enroll in a self-defense training program so I would never be victimized again.

I was not even 10 years old, and I went to self-defense training every day after school. The instructors shared alarming statistics about people caught up in cycles of abuse. They told us that abused children were 80 percent more likely to choose abusive adult partners and become victims of domestic violence. They also said abused children were 10 times more likely to use drugs and alcohol to cope with personal trauma. Then, they shared the good news that we didn't have to become those statistics. The class would teach us how to beat the odds.

No Means No

During class, instructors worked to restore our self-confidence. I learned techniques on how to speak up for myself and how to say *"No!"* I was taught verbal and mental, as well as physical, techniques for responding to potential threats. The instructors told us to always speak up and say our mind, to be bold and courageous. They drilled this point into us. We practiced saying *"No!"* over and over again. We said *"No!"* to anyone who tried to touch us. We said *"No!"* to anyone who tried to verbally put us down. We said *"No!"* in so many ways that it became a reflex in me.

After finishing the class, I was ready to take down the bad guys. I was only *nine years old, not even double digits,* but the renewed confidence changed my life forever. All that assertiveness training altered my little personality. I learned to speak my mind, and I was determined to speak up for other people.

The court also appointed a counselor for me at school, Ms. White. She was a kind woman who kept giving me messages of empowerment. She made me feel special because I was able to leave class whenever I needed to speak with her. On my last day of elementary school, she told me that I could help many people by sharing my story. I told her that I would help many people, but not by sharing my story.

Why would anyone want to know about the bad things that happened to me? I would be too busy doing good things to remember any of this.

What You Can Do

You may know someone who has experienced sexual violence or been discriminated against due to sexual orientation. There are no easy answers on how to end the problem, but here are some preventative measures based on my experience:

1. **Speak up.** Talk about sexual violence with your friends and family members. Explain that sexual violence is about power dynamics and social relations, not pleasure. Help people understand that abuse is not their fault. Encourage people to tell someone they can trust if something bad happens.
2. **Look for the warning signs.** Statistics show that women and children are more likely to be abused by someone they know than by strangers. If you see an odd behavior in a child or hear abusive words from

an adult, say something. Report suspected cases to the appropriate authority.

3. **Be prepared to act.** If you see someone being attacked, try to stop the perpetrator by making loud noises and getting people around you to help. Call social services and stand by the victim. Be willing to take someone to the hospital, listen to a story, and offer your support.

4. **Don't treat survivors as victims.** If you know a survivor, don't stereotype or pity them. They can be powerful agents of change by helping to end the cycle of violence. Offer encouraging words and messages of empowerment.

5. **Men can champion women's rights as caring friends, coworkers, and life partners.** Help redefine masculinity beyond paradigms of power and control. Reinforce the message that strong men don't physically hurt or verbally abuse women. Don't discriminate, implicitly or tacitly. Allow men and women to express their gender identities with full respect for their human rights and basic freedoms.

Remember, you have the power to protect people from harm. By being aware of the needs around you and being ready to act when the situation arises, you can change a life. **When you change one life, you will see that you, too, can change the world.**

7

PROTECTING PEOPLE

"Security is mostly a superstition. It does not exist in nature, nor do the children of men as a whole experience it. Avoiding danger is no safer in the long run than outright exposure. Life is either a daring adventure, or nothing."

Helen Keller, deaf-blind author and activist

Protecting people is my mission in life. It is my calling. You may be wondering: what does it mean exactly, to protect someone?

It is about keeping them safe from harm.

In a humanitarian context, offering protection can mean different things depending, of course, on different situations. In natural disasters, protecting people can mean providing them with access to their essential needs by giving aid. In war zones, protecting people is about physical safety from harm, mostly from armed groups who are fighting.

In both conflict and disaster situations, a fundamental aspect of protection is ensuring that the human rights of those affected are respected by the authorities who have a responsibility to provide for the people. Protection is ultimately, therefore, about governance and ensuring that leaders act responsibly to provide for the safety, dignity, and well-being of the population.

International organizations define humanitarian protection as:

All activities aimed at obtaining full respect for the rights of the individual in accordance with the letter and the spirit of relevant bodies of human rights, humanitarian and refugee law.[27]

The rule of law holds authorities accountable to protect people from inhumane treatment, violence, deprivation of liberty, lack of freedom of movement, and other forms of human rights abuses, such as torture. Denying people their basic need for food, water, and shelter is also an abuse. Ensuring that people have access to these rights, and to humanitarian assistance, is a major aspect of humanitarian work. Providing for the physical safety of people under threat of violence is another matter.

When I first learned about the legal protections that refugees and displaced people have according to international law, it seemed like something important was missing. What about physical protection from danger? How was the law going to keep armed groups from killing civilians and one another? How can we keep terrorists with weapons from enslaving women and forcibly recruiting child soldiers?

This lack of physical protection from harm seemed like a big gap. When I asked my colleagues about it, they would say,

"Physical protection is the responsibility of national governments. We are to hold them accountable."

---

[27]See the UN Office for the Coordination of Humanitarian Affairs (OCHA) Brief, *What is protection?* https://www.unocha.org/

National authorities are comprised of governments and armed forces, including police and military forces that would, ideally, protect their people from harm. Yet, in many contexts weak and failing states have a difficult time providing public safety and basic administrative functions throughout the country. Competition over economic and environmental resources, including land and water, can lead to social conflict between groups. If grievances go unaddressed, they can boil over into a full-scale conflict. In some traditional societies, informal dispute resolution mechanisms exist that keep communities from fighting with one another. Effective national governments also have functional judicial systems that offer recourse for wrongdoing in a court of law. However, in many contexts, national authorities fail to provide mechanisms for reconciling competing interests. When these groups become armed, violence ensues.

Responsibility to Protect (R2P)

The international community, as ambiguous as the term may seem, is comprised of nations working together for peace and security. The United Nations is the lead agency working toward peace in many parts of the world, addressing gaps in governance and conflict resolution as well as meeting humanitarian needs. Today, regional bodies like the African Union (AU), Arab League, European Union (EU), and Association of Southeast Asian Nations (ASEAN), among others, have enormous influence over regional problems, including negotiating peace agreements and authorizing multi-national operations to provide security in weak and failing states.

In response to the genocide and ethnic cleansing that occurred in Rwanda and the Balkans in the 1990s, the

Government of Canada led a study on the Responsibility to Protect (R2P), outlining the case for international intervention when states failed to protect their people from harm. The report produced by the International Commission on Intervention and State Sovereignty outlined three core aspects of this responsibility:

1. **Responsibility to prevent** harm before it occurs through early warning
2. **Responsibility to react,** which is largely seen as a decision to intervene
3. **Responsibility to rebuild** after an intervention has occurred

These findings have been fiercely debated in the United Nations Security Council ever since. While most countries agree that there is a responsibility to prevent violence, some nations are reluctant to intervene in national affairs, notably China and Russia, who often veto decisions to intervene in places like Darfur, Sudan, where ethnic cleansing began in 2004. In 2009, the International Criminal Court issued a warrant to arrest President al-Bashir for war crimes and crimes against humanity in Darfur.

The United Nations

While the UN Security Council has used its authority to launch peacekeeping missions with a mandate to protect civilians from harm since 1999, the R2P agenda has largely failed to galvanize authoritarian regimes to change their behavior. This is particularly true on UN resolutions related to Syria and North Korea, whose governments have continued to oppress their people with little recourse.

Countries have also had a difficult time rallying around the responsibility to rebuild nations torn apart by war. Even after the United Nations and NATO were united in their effort to intervene in Libya when Muammar Gaddafi vowed *"to cleanse Libya from house to house"* like rats, the military campaign to protect the Libyan people only lasted until Gaddafi was deposed. After several weeks of air campaigns, NATO ended the mission. There were no efforts to rebuild Libya. More importantly, there was no effort to disarm radical militias who continued to perpetuate violence against the population. Those same militias are fighting in Libya today.[28]

This information is important for you to know because as someone who is preparing to work on the ground in crisis, you have to maintain awareness of what is happening behind the scenes. It's important to understand who is fighting and what fuels the conflict in order to bring about peace. For every country in crisis, the international community is working to restore order and bring about peace. Just as you are trying to address the suffering on the ground, which is the visible manifestation of the conflict or disaster, nations are working together to address the root causes and overcome the source of instability.

This is the core mission of the United Nations, which provides immeasurable value to all people, despite its flaws, in its quest to bring about conditions of global peace and security. Just as you will face limitations on what you can do in reality, the UN is an institution with limited power. It depends on the collective will of the nations for its decision-making authority.

---

[28]For more information about the NATO mission in Libya, see my paper *Overcoming Protection of Civilians Failures: The Case for an Evolutionary Approach in NATO*, OPEN Publications, Volume 1 Number 4, Spring 2017.

However, its purposes, as enshrined by its 1945 founding charter, remain noble:[29]

- To save future generations from the scourge of war
- To reaffirm faith in human rights, in the dignity and worth of the human person, and in the equal rights of men and women
- To practice tolerance and live together in peace with one another as good neighbors
- To unite our strength to maintain international peace and security

Outside the UN building in New York City, you will find a bronze statue of the barrel of a gun that has been twisted into knots, *The Knotted Gun* by Swedish artist Carl Fredrik. One block away, in a small park by a fountain, this scripture is inscribed into the wall:

> *"and they shall beat their swords into plowshares and their spears into pruning hooks; Nation shall not lift up sword against nation, neither shall they learn war anymore."*
>
> Isaiah 2:4

Human Security

There are theories about how to conduct "just wars" and laws about the conduct of war. But as a whole, humanity is not served by war. Rather, humanity is served when people are free to reach their full potential. In order to have this freedom, people need their basic needs met. They need more than an end

---

[29]Read the full United Nations Charter here, https://www.un.org/en/sections/un-charter/preamble/index.html

to war. They need conditions that allow for human security. Here's how one woman describes it:

"When we talk security as women, we're talking human security. It's not about the guns. . . It's about our life, food, education and health."

> *Priscilla Joseph, Founder and Chairperson South Sudan Women's Peace Network*[30]

The concept of human security was formally recognized by the United Nations General Assembly in 2012 as a way of holding states accountable for the well-being of their populations. It described *human security as being able to meet seven essential needs*: 1) economic 2) health 3) personal 4) political 5) food 6) environmental and 7) communal security.

This idea was based on former U.S. President Roosevelt in his 1941 address to Congress, urging the United States to stop German Chancellor Adolf Hitler and his Nazi party from taking over Europe. In his speech, Roosevelt claimed that all people have *Four Freedoms: freedom from want, freedom from fear, freedom of speech, and freedom of religion.* He urged the United States to join with the international community in preserving these freedoms for all people.

Today, human security is recognized as an approach that puts individual security at the core of protection efforts. Traditional notions of security refer to national security and the various apparatuses of control that belong to nation-states, including administrative, financial, and security functions. Human security recognizes the importance of securing the

---

[30]See the Council on Foreign Relations report, Women's Roles In Brief: South Sudan, 2020. https://www.cfr.org/interactive/interactive/womens-participation-in-peace-processes/south-sudan-0

individual, households, and communities so they can live in safety and with dignity. The human security framework offers governments the essential criteria for meeting basic needs and achieving human development.

Solutions to Insecurity

According to the World Bank, half of all people living in extreme poverty also live in fragile state contexts.[31] In the absence of responsible government authorities, humanitarian and development agencies fill critical gaps in meeting people's needs. Oftentimes, this goes far beyond the normal activities of providing basic items like food and shelter to those in distress. Aid can also take on more complex forms, such as strengthening systems that provide clean water, sanitation and hygiene facilities, waste cleanup and debris removal, and other administrative functions like resolving land disputes and establishing informal banking mechanisms, as well as replacing judicial and financial institutions that are inexistent or poorly functioning.

In complex environments, humanitarians fill many gaps that would otherwise be the responsibility of the government. However, humanitarians do not have the authority to address *gaps in physical safety and public order*. This is the responsibility of the security sector, which includes police, military, and other uniformed services. These security sector "actors" should be under the control of democratically elected governments.

Community leaders also play a role in keeping people safe at the local level. However, stopping the violence is difficult when

---

[31]See World Bank Fragility, Conflict and Violence (FCV) Strategy 2020-2025, February 27, 2020.

the root causes of the conflict are not being addressed at the political level. It is even more difficult when the warring parties have significant control of people, land, and resources. In such cases, warring parties may not have an incentive to stop fighting.

In areas of active conflict, where violence is ongoing, agencies work on mitigating risks to different types of groups, determining the threats people face by age, gender, and other social factors, such as each ethnic or linguistic identity. Protection activities include assessing risks; raising awareness of threats within the community; taking action that minimizes harm; providing safe spaces for those affected, such as refugee camps; and working with local authorities to hold perpetrators of violence accountable for their actions. Effective protection enables and empowers communities affected by violence to better protect themselves and provide for their own needs.

Protection of Civilians

In the context of war, protecting civilians is of paramount importance. There are over fifty active conflicts in the world today, ten of which are high-intensity, violent conflicts resulting in over 1,000 deaths a year.[32] Conflicts in Afghanistan, South Sudan, Yemen, Iraq, and Syria are highly complex emergencies, affecting millions of people.

In the last ten years, 2.5 million people have died as a result of war.[33] Conflict changes people's normal patterns of life, resulting in a "new normal" focused entirely on survival. In every country, people have a daily routine and normal pattern of life. Each morning, adults wake up, go to work,

---

[32]Alert Annual Report on Conflict, 2019.
[33]Uppsala Conflict Data Program (UCDP), 2020.

and send their children to school. In countries that have an agrarian-based economy, many people are involved in agricultural work. This involves planting and harvesting crops, then transporting produce to sell at nearby markets.

In a war zone, it is often unsafe to work outside in the fields. When there is active fighting, soldiers may be on the roads that farmers use to transport crops to market. This leads to a slowdown in the production of food, causing many people to go hungry. Children may be killed by snipers or aerial bombs on their way to school. Women can be targeted or raped on the way to market.

When the patterns of life become compromised by the presence of armed groups, everything becomes more difficult for civilians. When adults can no longer work or bring food home to their families or when children can no longer go to school safely, this is when the risk of violence becomes too much for people to bear. This perpetual fear and insecurity during conflict is what forces people to leave their homes, migrate to a safer town, or leave the country entirely, becoming refugees.

"Human security is a term which carries the risk of meaning all and nothing. This is why I would like to put it into a context, and I will do so by referring essentially to the experience of protecting and assisting refugees.

The importance of human security as a concept is clear if you consider that (sic) refugees are people who are, by definition, "insecure." Refugees and internally displaced people are a significant symptom of human insecurity crises. Because homes, personal belongings and family ties are such an important part of everybody's security,

*it takes considerable pressure to force people to aban-
don them and become refugees.*"

*Sadako Ogata, Former UN High
Commissioner for Refugees*

Because of their vulnerability, refugees have special protection under international law. When people flee their home
country, seeking protection in another country, their right to
seek asylum is part of the UN Refugee Convention of 1951.
The convention was adopted after Jewish survivors of the
Holocaust fled Europe, fearing for their lives. There are over
26 million refugees living outside their home country and 45
million internally displaced persons (IDPs) who are in their
own country but cannot go home.[34] These are people who,
due to a well-founded fear of persecution, need a new place to
call home.

War puts people in harm's way. Those who do not bear
arms or engage in fighting are called *civilians*. According to the
Geneva Conventions, civilians and civilian objects like schools,
hospitals, and humanitarian workers are to be protected.
Although civilians are not a legitimate target, armed groups
both accidentally and intentionally target them during conflict,
resulting in thousands of deaths and injuries in war zones.

According to the Law of Armed Conflict (LOAC), soldiers
wearing a uniform that represents their national military are in
a different category. They are considered to be lawful *combat-
ants*, which makes them legitimate military targets by opposing
forces. These soldiers are under the protection of a legitimate

---

[34]UNHCR, Figures at a Glance, as of June 2020.

government that authorizes the use of force in an international conflict.

However, terrorist groups and non-state actors are hard to define because they do not wear a uniform, and they do not belong to any one country. They do not always fall under a state or national authority structure. Many armed groups operate through subnational and local structures, including criminal gangs and syndicates. Irregular fighters without national authority are considered to be *belligerents* according to the laws of war.

These distinctions are outlined in more detail in International Humanitarian Law (IHL) and International Human Rights Law (IHRL), which offer fundamental protections for civilians regardless of who is fighting, including protection from arbitrary detention and loss of life, from torture, and from other forms of ill and degrading treatment. Yet, armed groups intentionally co-locate and intermix with civilians as a deliberate strategy to avoid targeting.

This matters to you because the law states that the military and armed groups are not allowed to target civilians, yet many innocent people die in war. Some militaries view this "collateral damage" as an inevitable consequence of war. But it doesn't have to be this way.

Protect the People

When humanitarian agencies and armed actors work together on protecting civilians from harm, they bring two important approaches together. The first approach uses humanitarian protection assessments to determine the risks to the population and how to minimize harm to each group based on their specific demographics. The second approach is based on military intelligence that analyses the intent and capability of perpetrators to harm those groups of people. In conflict zones, these approaches operate in silos, both having critical information that, if shared, could save lives and reduce human suffering.

That's why I formed an organization called Protect the People, to build bridges between humanitarians and the military. I wanted to bring together humanitarian and military approaches to protect people in danger.

When I formed the organization, I brought together a network of experts to advise governments and militaries on the best approach to minimize harm to civilians. The network was made up of experts with decades of experience in emergency response and security sector cooperation.

Together, the network worked to bridge the gap I had identified. We worked on incredible projects, assessing the needs of people in Syria and Yemen, mapping local networks of civil society organizations that could provide aid in hard-to-reach areas. We trained military and police personnel on improving civil-military coordination, working with contingents going into United Nations peacekeeping operations and NATO missions. We also provided training for U.S. military forces, testing their capabilities for responding to complex emergencies.

Protect the People raised the bar on international standards for the protection of civilians. In this capacity, I contributed to the development of U.S. Army and Joint military doctrine on the protection of civilians and mass atrocity response operations that included protection from physical violence and contributed to a safe and secure environment for civilians. I also worked with NATO on guidance to protect civilians that was approved by all twenty-nine ministries of defense within the alliance. This involved helping many forces conceptualize not only *what is protection*, but *how to protect* people in operations. This included designing numerous trainings and war games to help military and police forces understand risks to civilians and how to keep them out of harm's way.

I am sharing this with you so that you can see the link between the seemingly small things you do to help each person you meet and the big picture of achieving global change.

The work you start off doing as a helper won't be where you end up. The more experience you have with people in your field, the more you will want to address issues at the source of the problems you see in the world. Your life's work can be a game changer for people in need. Even now, you can do great things for humanity.

Idealism vs. Realism

In this work, I have found that there is a disconnect between the goal we set out to achieve, namely, to relieve suffering, and what is reality on the ground, which shows the obvious human deprivation and destruction in tough places like Syria, Haiti, and the Congo.

The truth is, it's a lot easier to say that something needs to be done, to make a speech at an international conference or write a post on social media, than to find a way to save lives on the ground.

That is why you are needed. The humanitarian sector needs contributions from new people with fresh ideas—it also needs to capture the imagination of political leaders and donors to

help them envision a better future for civilians caught up in conflict.

Your desire to help can and will contribute to a better world. Don't let anyone tell you differently. You only need to apply yourself to the needs you see and get out there. I have found ways to close the gaps by working on operations that have *the potential to save lives* and reduce the likelihood of bad things happening to people.

Over the course of my career, I have worked on the ground with small amounts of money to help a few people, and I have worked in command centers training forces going into battle. This ability to influence the actions of others, to analyze threats and offer courses of action to keep people safe, allows me to see that protection can be achieved in both big and small ways.

Oftentimes, the best thing that humanitarians can do in the absence of government responsibility is to hold authorities accountable for their actions. Sometimes we will achieve amazing results, such as negotiating ceasefires between warring parties that allow civilians to evacuate the area, and sometimes we can only point people toward the goal, arguing that people have a right to assistance and protection and that this right supersedes other political objectives.

How do you know that what you do saves lives?

The more you work toward the goal of making the world a better place, the more you will see what is possible. Keep your eyes set on the vision of what you are being called to do.

Be a force for good in the world. You can make a difference by offering your everyday self to the situation at hand. You don't have to be in a powerful position to start making a difference. Your efforts can improve situations that once seemed impossible. Even if you cannot save every life, save the life that you can. Each step you take toward the goal of helping humanity is important. Start now.

8

KEEPING FAITH IN HUMANITY

"For God does speak—now one way, now another—though no one perceives it. In a dream, in a vision of the night, when deep sleep falls on people as they slumber in their beds, he may speak in their ears."

Job 33: 14-16

Faith in Humanity

Humanitarian work requires an active belief in the power of humanity to prevail through the most difficult of circumstances. This belief comes in many forms, shapes, and sizes. The largest of these is 2.3 billion followers of Christianity, followed by 1.9 billion who profess Islam, and another billion secularists who profess no faith at all.[35] This chapter is going to focus on the importance of cultivating a spiritual life, particularly as you deal with matters of life and death.

I grew up in the Christian tradition, and even as a young girl, I had a sense that God was real. The Bible says *that faith is being sure of what we hope for and certain of what we do*

---

[35]Figures are from the Pew-Templeton Global Religious Futures Project as of 2020, and research by Dr. Juan Stephen, anthropologist at the University of Sydney, Australia.

not see. It's the complete opposite of the popular saying, *seeing is believing.* When you're confronted with people who are suffering, faith is about believing that good will prevail, even when you only see bad things in front of you.

My faith has given me the strength to actively intervene on behalf of people in crisis and to boldly confront obstacles to meeting their needs. Whether you practice a religion or have no faith at all, I hope this chapter encourages you to see the power of the human spirit expressed throughout the world.

Anticipating Needs

While doing relief work, you see many problems that don't have easy answers. For example, you want to get nutritional supplements to a malnourished child barely able to feed from his mother's breast. You desperately want that child to stay alive. You hope that the shipment of supplies coming into the port is going to arrive on time so the child can live. You hope that criminal gangs won't steal your supplies while they are in transit, that they won't get lost or stolen by warring parties or become spoiled by poor road and weather conditions.

You really want that shipment to come through, so instead of going about your routine the day it's supposed to come in, you go to the port yourself and make sure that customs are prepared to release it directly to your organization. You take the nutritional supplement directly to the clinic because you know it will save the child's life. This is being sure of what you hope for—that by being proactive, you will save the child's life. This, too, is an act of faith.

You see needs of refugees, people on the move who are not in their own country, which are hard to meet. You come across a young refugee dying of HIV/AIDS, but the anti-retroviral drugs to help him cost more than your program budget allows you to spend. You could refer him to a local clinic, but many health care providers do not serve foreigners. Even though treating people with HIV/AIDS is not your core mission, you don't let that stop you from finding a solution. You work to negotiate a better price, buying down the cost of the drug from pharmaceutical companies, until you can get the young man what he needs.

You know there are more young men like him who also need drug treatment to stay alive, so you negotiate a bulk price for an estimated number of people who are likely to contract the virus. That way, whenever a case of HIV shows up, you are better prepared to meet that need. This is being certain of what you do not see, projecting into future needs and preparing in advance to do the work ahead. This foresight is also an act of faith.

Kandahar

Then, there are times and places where circumstances are so overwhelming, you know that short-term relief is a drop in the bucket compared to the magnitude of the problem. That's how I felt when I first landed in Kandahar, Afghanistan after the September 11, 2001 terrorist attack in the United States.

From the moment I arrived, I knew I was in a war zone. As our small United Nations airplane flew from the capital city of Kabul to Kandahar in the south, the Hindu Kush Mountains looked like a vast ocean of endless high peaks. When the plane landed, all I could see was sand whirling around the plane until the pilot came on the speaker with a special announcement:

"Folks, we've been instructed not to deplane until further notice. Please remain seated."

I looked out the window of the plane. As the sand blowing across the desert settled, *I saw men in black with weapons attached to every part of their body, surrounding our small plane.* Even their faces were covered in black ski masks, so we could not identify them.

Then I saw a large aircraft come in for a landing beside our meager aircraft. When it opened its hull, the aircraft looked like a warship, like the Star Trek enterprise was opening to let in another aircraft. Then, a line of men bound in chains emerged from another building. The men in black left our plane to surround the shackled men as they were loaded onto the aircraft. The shackled men were wearing orange jumpsuits, and their faces were covered with hoods. They were prisoners. The U.S. was taking them to Guantanamo prison in Cuba.

When we finally deplaned, I saw that U.S. military forces had painted a shark across the top of the airport. It said, *"You are safe here,"* and the shark was smiling. I wasn't so sure whether anyone was safe here. *How could people be so dangerous that they had to be chained together and hauled away to a remote island?*

Truly, to my eyes, *this place seemed like another world.*

In the small desert town of Kandahar that served as a regional hub for trade, I lived in a secure compound not far from my office. Soon after my arrival, I saw a group of women walking down the road, covered from head to toe in blue *burkas* (which made it impossible to see any part of their body). They were carrying heavy bags of food rations from an aid distribution site on their heads. Seeing them struggle with their heavy loads, with one hand on their head and another trying to lift the hem of the *burka* so they would not trip as they struggled to walk, I cried.

The women were carrying a heavy load because conditions were bad. These were the same women I had read about in college who were forced to watch the Taliban stone other women to death for reading books, going to school, or committing adultery. Even though the Taliban was on its way out, the women were hardly liberated. They had endured seven years of drought which made it hard to feed their families, and they continued to suffer violence from within their own families.

During the day, *I spent long hours counting the people in need with my fellow aid workers. How many women lost their husbands and brothers in the fighting? How many elderly people needed medical attention? How many children did not have parents or adults with them? How many young men were missing since the fighting began?*

We asked questions and we counted, then we turned these numbers into assessments on the conditions of those affected by war. The assessments became written proposals for funding to establish programs to meet the needs of each specific group of people.

Dreams and Visions

We moved from one camp of displaced people to the next, seeing thousands of people every day, but at night the roads were blocked by checkpoints. We were not allowed to go out past dark. Every night, I would fall into bed exhausted. The days blended together in a dusty haze. A day felt like a week, a week felt like a month. When I fell asleep, I would dream....

I was a bird, soaring high above the desert. From the air, I could see all the people down below. With my vast wings and small body, I could soar easily in and out of the clouds and over the mountains. I could fly, undetected. No one could see me, but I could see everything and everyone down below.

Having greater ability to see, I could account for all the people down below. I surveyed the number of homes in the town, the number of cars moving through the streets, how many people traveled by foot, and the number of refugees living in rows of tents organized by the United Nations.

I could finally see the whole picture when the clouds erupted. Large drops of dew formed and fell from the sky. I could feel the damp raindrops on my wings—then rain! When the people felt water falling from the sky, they stopped moving. They stopped everything they were doing. They held out their hands, their lips, their tongues.

Could it be true, that it was raining in Kandahar?

Like a long-awaited guest, people came out of their houses to greet it, to see if it was really there. Indeed, it was raining. Women went back into their homes to gather buckets. Children started dancing in the streets. Men gazed up at the sky in disbelief. Then...

I woke up. I was in my bed; I was no longer a bird. The air was bone dry. I climbed up to the roof. There was no sign of rain on the horizon. I went to the kitchen to make coffee. Our cook was humming quietly.

I asked him, "Amadou, how long has it been since it rained here?"

"I don't know, Miss Sarah. A long time."

"How long?" I asked.

"At least seven years," he said. "Long time," he said again, shaking his head in sadness.

"When do you think it will rain again?"

"No one knows but Allah. God willing, the rain will come again, *Inshallah*."

That night, I prayed for the dream to be real. I prayed for the people who needed food and a safe place to live. I prayed for protection for the people I could not reach. I prayed for God to relieve the suffering and endless need.

Rain for Kandahar

I had to leave Afghanistan for a few days in order to buy supplies in Pakistan. Winter was coming, and we would need blankets and shawls to keep people warm in the tent cities.

This time, as my plane returned to Kandahar, there was no sandstorm or prisoners being transported. But something even stranger was happening. Dew drops formed on the airplane window. Rain had come to Kandahar at last.

As I rode back into town, people were celebrating, just as they were in my dream. Divine intervention showed up, providing a form of relief greater than anything I could do. The sky had opened up, and it was raining for the first time in seven years—it was truly miraculous.

Seeing from Above

While I have not seen God, I have seen the work of God in every place I have been. Despite harsh words from political leaders espousing that some places are hopeless, *there are no forsaken places or forsaken people.* God will have mercy on whom he has mercy, and his kindness covers all people.

My work has allowed me to do great things, but my faith inspires me to believe in even greater things, to believe in miracles. The creator does not leave the created world defenseless; he guards and watches over it, like a garden that is being tended to with great care, like a watchman on guard.

As human beings, we have limited vision. We can only see what is right in front of us at any given time. The Bible says that *"we see in part and know in part,"* meaning that as humans we have limited understanding. We would therefore benefit from having humility as we consider the complexity of the world, leaving room for mystery and becoming comfortable with the unknown rather than having to explain everything.

Human beings cannot see behind or around us without special equipment. The disaster response community has developed early warning tracking tools and prediction models, but we cannot always predict what major world event will happen next.

At times, world events will be catastrophic—with deadly consequences. Daily, we see and hear about terrible things happening—people committing violent acts against other people, pandemics, wars, and natural disasters in which countless lives are threatened or lost. Yet, there is always something that can be done. In every situation, humanitarians are working to access people in need and deliver timely help.

A Spiritual Life

Whether you belong to a faith community or proclaim that you have no faith, your ability to cultivate a spiritual life is an important part of caring for yourself and others. Even if you reject organized religion, believing in and caring for humanity *is a courageous act of faith.* In this chapter, I want to suggest ways that faith can help you in this challenging business of humanitarian work.

> *"I see God in every human being. Not all of us can do great things, but we can do small things with great love."*
>
> Mother Teresa

Giving yourself to the many needs you see in the world can be exhausting. Without something deeper, stronger, and more inwardly life-giving than a desire to help people, it is easy to become cynical and jaded. In order not to give up, you need to be replenished and fulfilled from the core of your being.

This is where a greater force comes in—the strength that comes from faith.

You may be wondering: what good is faith in a difficult world? Faith provides us with hope in a better future not only for our lives but for people we see in need around us. It offers us perspective for seeing the big picture even when we can only see a small part of what is going on wherever we are at the moment.

Too often, we think of faith only in terms of adherence to a certain slate of doctrinal beliefs. It can be that—and it can be much, much more. For me, *it is more.* Faith is life and breath; it is a way of being that acknowledges each person has inherent worth and dignity, just as they are.

Faith informs my view of the world. Despite the bad things we see on the news, I am sure that the world is good. Even in the worst circumstances, when people have lost everything, I am certain there is a hope in the future for them. God sees the needs of all people. Faith calls me to believe that even when I don't see immediate changes at hand, I know that my actions to step forward and do something about it are part of a greater work being done in the world.

Faith counters the negative influences that show us the most terrible things—events that can, without faith, drain the heart and soul of human kindness. Faith gives me *hope for humanity* and emboldens me, assuring me that my work is about more than self-gratification. Helping is about loving. It is about loving life, loving people, and loving the world that God has made.

> *"The principle of humanity involves love in the deepest sense. Humanitarian action is an attention born of love for one another, and at its best, is a manifestation of love that respects, cares, understands, and responds."*
>
> *Hugo Slim*
> *International Committee of the Red Cross (ICRC)*

No matter how experienced you become in humanitarian work, every crisis will test your ability to respond to extremities that can pull you down. Each situation you face will require you to carefully observe the situation at hand and to develop creative, timely solutions with a diverse team of people. In every assignment, you are presented with new challenges: the culture of the people, the language, the vulnerability of each person and how they are being attacked, and the mechanisms available to protect them from harm. You will be challenged by the question of what to do and by the reality of what you cannot do but wish you could.

Faith offers us a path to the spiritual practice of being present with other people. Being with those who suffer as a loving, caring presence gives us a way to offer them hope. Having faith in a God who created the whole world, full of diversity in its people and expressions of life, means embracing people who are different, not just people who look and talk like you. **Believing in the power of humanity requires you to radically embrace all people, regardless of their religious beliefs.**

I must say, this kind of faith in the big picture and all humanity goes beyond what some traditions teach about individual faith. In some traditions, personal salvation is emphasized to the detriment of considering how God is at work in all people. When the circumstances of the world around you seem overwhelming, when children are dying and bodies are burning, you need a faith that's bigger than yourself. God is not only at work in you, the divine spirit is at work in the world despite the difficulties you see. The Creator sees humankind and is intervening in ways beyond our individual ability. My faith enables me to trust there is a path forward, even when I cannot see the whole picture, both for my life and for humanity as a whole.

The Value of Faith

Faith allows me to believe that God is present with each person and can work through anyone, in any situation at all times.

While gaining technical knowledge and training is important for your work, helping people requires you to keep an open mind. You need to remain flexible to find solutions that are outside the box. Working among people with different backgrounds is helpful to thinking through complex problems, and diverse perspectives are to be celebrated. People come in every shape, size, color, and belief system.

I've learned that everyone has something to contribute when people's lives are on the line. Dealing with complex problems means there are no easy answers. Knowing how to mobilize people and to work within diverse teams, including people of all faiths, is critical to getting the job done.

Experience has taught me that being in close proximity to people in crisis makes a huge difference in my work. Sitting in a distant office making decisions based on policy alone usually doesn't produce a solution to people's problems. Going on mission is key to understanding the unique needs in each environment. There is no substitute for the experience that comes from working with affected populations and local communities to find solutions on the ground. Though it may be difficult to reach people in a crisis situation, being in direct contact with those affected is critical to assessing their needs.

Sometimes, however, you cannot be present where people are suffering. You may not be able to access people who are besieged in a war zone. As you become more senior in the field, you are likely to supervise a team of people in an office at agency headquarters or be fundraising for country programs. Even when you are not "on assignment" or "in the field," it is still possible to be in solidarity with those whom you are serving—in a spiritual way.

One way I do this is through prayer. When I cannot be physically present with people in danger, I pray that they will find a way out and that their instincts would guide them to safety.

Every time I see a large storm about to hit, I pray for the people in its path. When I saw Hurricane Katrina about to hit New Orleans, I prayed for the people who would be inundated by the storm waters. When the levees broke, I prayed that I would be sent to help. Within days, my boss got a call from the White House asking her to send me down.

After an earthquake struck Haiti in 2010, I knew that I would be going to help as soon as transportation could be arranged. I prayed for a way to access local organizations who were affected. Even though phone lines were down, I was able to get an email through to Haitian organizations who could clearly express what they needed so I could prepare appropriately. Within days, I was on my way to the epicenter of the crisis.

Offering Your Life in Service

You can also practice prayer through mindfulness, meditating on the needs you see and seeking clarity on what you can do in response. These prayers for the people, and for God to make a way for you to help, may seem simple. What the prayers are really asking for is for your life to be an offering.

Your life is the greatest gift you can give to humanity. Cultivating a unique skill set so you are prepared to respond to the needs of the world and having a mindset of preparedness so that you are willing to go when called will help you be ready when the opportunity comes.

When you arrive on assignment, you also have to be bold to get things done. This boldness is also a matter of faith, believing that you can overcome any obstacle. Being insistent is often the only way to make things happen in a chaotic environment. Personal perseverance and fortitude are critical to reducing the suffering of others. If helping people were easy, then no one would be in need anymore. But it is hard work that requires "grit." Grit is about being determined, even when circumstances throw obstacles your way.

When I am on mission, knowing that I am living out my calling, I will stop at nothing to get things done. In the Dominican Republic, I hired a local fixer to help me bargain with customs to release tents I had shipped down to Haiti. The tents were for the staff members of a local NGO who were made homeless by the quake. They were living on the streets, and I knew that once I could get their needs met, the staff would be back up and running, helping many more people.

Even though I don't speak Spanish and my fixer didn't speak English, I learned to speak to him through gestures and drawings until he could understand what I needed to communicate to customs officials. We waited outside the customs office every day until the papers were signed to release the tents. Once the situation was resolved, I would never see that fixer again, but I would always be grateful for how he helped me resolve the situation.

The truth is, you have to be insistent to get supplies to people when they need them most. Sometimes you have to fight the very system set up to help people. At the onset of winter in Afghanistan, babies started dying of extremely cold temperatures. Even though I purchased supplies in Pakistan, there weren't enough blankets to reach every family living in a tent.

However, *there were* piles of heavy blankets in UN warehouses waiting to be distributed to another project. I asked to have additional blankets for the children under five who were dying from the cold. To my surprise, the head of the warehouse said no, and the head of the supply unit said no. Those blankets were set aside for another project. So, I went to the head of the office responsible for the warehouse, and I made the case to their leadership.

"The warehouse can be resupplied," I insisted.

"Babies are dying every day. We can't get their lives back once they are lost."

Trying to appeal to his self-interest, I told him, *"Look, it's all over the news. This is a bad news story. We can turn it into a good story."*

After appealing the initial decision, the head of supplies modified my program budget to reflect the cost of additional blankets. As a result, dozens of babies in the camps were saved that winter. Helping people requires personal determination, perseverance, and fortitude. It requires faith in your ability to get things done and working hard until you achieve the intended result.

Advocating for Refugees

When I moved back to Washington D.C., I brought this same boldness to advocating for refugees and displaced people to the U.S. Congress. Public policy can be a life or death matter for people that need immigration papers to leave their country in order to be safe.

At the time that I was evacuated out of Afghanistan in 2003, refugees from Muslim-majority countries were being denied visas to come to the United States. Even after the United Nations had designated them as urgent humanitarian cases, people could not get through the system because of their religion. Breaking through the gridlock that kept them from leaving could save their lives.

I wanted to help these special cases be considered for resettlement. This would get them out from living under a tent, enable them to get on a diet of real food instead of living on meager food rations, and allow them to be reunited with family. Decisions from a government agency could either change their lives or keep them waiting in line.

I tried to make government officials understand that they had power to grant people life-saving assistance, whether that was in the form of special immigrant status or providing funding so that more aid could reach more people.

All of this work took faith—great leaps of faith. Sometimes I would argue for more funding. Other times, I would advocate for a population to be considered for resettlement to another country. I often wasn't sure whether all this advocacy—beseeching authorities and appealing to their sense of goodwill—would work out. I wasn't sure if Republicans and Democrats would come together to help people halfway around the world. I wasn't sure whether the right argument was one of compassion, that the U.S. has a history of welcoming refugees since the end of World War II, or one of expediency, that it was cheaper to offer a refugee a new home country than pay for them to receive handouts in far-off camps for the rest of their lives. Both arguments were true and called for creative solutions to resolve refugee crisis.

Guidance from Above

Faith is also believing that God will show up when there is an unexpected need. I have not seen God, but I have seen God show up in the hands and feet of other people. I saw God in a refugee camp when I came upon a sick man no one could move to a far-away clinic. Then, ten minutes later, a doctor from another organization came up to me, asking if anyone in the camp needed medical attention. She showed up right on time.

Likewise, weeks after the Haiti earthquake, I went to a densely forested area where I suspected there might be people needing help that went undetected by satellite imagery. I met a young girl whose leg was crushed by the rubble. She rested under a tree and never received care. Her wound became infected, and I didn't think she would make it if my team took her to the clinic by our office, which was an hour away. So, we stood by the side of the road, trying to hail down a truck.

Even though we were in a remote location, a truck with an empty bed came by within five minutes. The driver of the truck was willing to transport her to the nearest hospital. You can call that luck or circumstance, but I believe it is God at work, wanting every person who is hurting to be seen and to be healed. ***There are no coincidences.***

In case you're wondering, I have not heard God speak audibly. But I have learned how to listen for the voice of his Spirit, in a whisper or an inclination of knowledge. After all, God is not limited by my distractions or my inability to pick up certain signals. Sometimes he speaks through our subconscious, through dreams and visions.

Dreams have been a guiding force for my life, and I came to believe long ago that a spiritual presence is communicating with me through them, as with others before me. You may not have experienced dreams in this way, or you may be skeptical of their ability to provide direction over the course of your life. The following dreams that I am sharing with you have expressed my deep desire to do things for people that I could not achieve in reality. They also revealed the hope within me when I felt a deep loss.

The Garden

In college, for instance, I had a dream that I was looking out over a large valley surrounded by mountains.

I was soaring above many plots of land with a large bird guiding me along the way. Each plot of land in the valley belonged to someone; each plot represented someone's life.

A great spirit hovered above the gardens, watching over them. The bird led me to a plot of land that seemed to belong to me. Once I was in the garden, a man came alongside me. He walked me around my plot, explaining it to me.

"This is your garden," he said. "It represents everything in your life, from birth to death." I looked around the plot carefully. There was beauty and there was sadness. There were things that were growing and dying, all under the same conditions.

Suddenly, I became upset about the parts of the garden that had died. The man, feeling my concern, came closer and assured me that my garden was good. For a brief moment, my eyes were opened to everything the garden represented. I was full of knowledge, and I was pleased with my life....

When I woke up, I could no longer remember what the garden represented, only that it was beautiful, and it seemed so very real.

I believe I was shown these things so I would know that no matter what comes my way, life is ultimately good. I can embrace the suffering I see in the world in the same

way that I accept a painful loss in my own life—by believing that new life is coming into being.

I also dream about people around the world who are endangered by conflict. I believe the dreams are prompting me to pray for them. I do not know whether the people I dream about are real or whether they represent a bigger reality that I have experienced in my work. Either way, I believe dreams are a way God urges us to live in solidarity with people who are suffering.

A Bird's Eye View

I had another dream about people from Myanmar after coming back from the tsunami response in Thailand. My mind was riddled with guilt that I could leave refugee children behind by getting on a plane, yet they could not leave their dismal conditions.

Refugees from Myanmar who were living in Thailand could not go home without facing a repressive military junta. The military dictatorship was halting attempts at political reform that would bring democracy to the country, including imprisoning renowned opposition leader Aung San Suu Kyi. Refugees were willing to put up with terrible conditions in Thailand that restricted their freedom to move and right to work, forcing them to live as second-class citizens. If conditions would change in Myanmar, the people could return home in safety. That's when I dreamt that I could help women and children still trapped inside the country.

In one dream, *I was a large bird with expansive wings, watching over people who were trapped by the militia.*

They knew they were in the middle of two armies, but they didn't know how close they were or when the fighting would begin. On one side of town, the military formed into a line with their weapons drawn. They were dressed in uniform, followed by a commander who assured their formation would give them a foothold on securing the town center.

Around the foothills of the lush jungle, loosely formed groups of rebel forces known as the junta were ready for battle. With their faces painted and spiritual emblems hanging from their necks, they not only looked fierce, they were deadly.

I could see the women and children running from one side of the street to another of the nearly deserted town. Most of the people who heard about the pending attack had already left town. But these five remained: two older women with three small children who didn't get out in time. They went one way, then another, not knowing where to go. They went from building to building seeking cover.

All at once, the dream grew more intense. The fighting was about to begin. The two forces drew near, one side letting out a battle cry, the other sounding a cannon.

Like a bird, I flew down from the air and came alongside the women and children. "Go this way—hide in here," I directed, pointing to a small home with tall, heavily draped windows that could hide them from sight. "Quick; follow me inside."

I showed the children how to hide by a window, wrapping themselves around the bottom of a long curtain. I tucked the women away behind the shutters of the doorway.

At that moment, the junta passed by the street in front of us, mere inches from the open window. The curtains blew in the wind from outside, but the children anchored the draped fabric down so that no one peering inside could see them. The house looked completely empty.

Suddenly, I heard crashing, and the soldiers came inside to search the house.

"Quiet," I whispered to the children, still soaring above them like a bird.

Then, my wings became like an invisible shield, causing the soldiers to pass on to other parts of the house. They peeked in the front room, where the women and children were hiding, then hesitated as if they were about to enter before moving to the next room.

When the junta and military forces left the area, I told the women and children to remain inside until they heard nothing at all. As I flew away, their eyes peered at me as if to ask, "What will happen to us now?"

I woke up, sweating. I knew I was being prompted to pray, and I did, fervently.

God be with the people of Myanmar who are under constant threat of violence. Help the women and children find a way out of the dangerous situations that pervade their lives. Grant them safety and give them a way out. Amen.

The Soldier

Here is another dream that I believe came from God.

After being evacuated out of Afghanistan, I thought about people in Kandahar every day. My team was still working, going out to the displaced persons camps. The biggest threat to their safety was being on the road where they could be ambushed by insurgents or their vehicles could be hit by explosives. They also came across Afghan soldiers and U.S. military forces every day as they tried to protect civilians from being caught in the crossfires of war.

That's when I had a dream—*that I was a bird flying high above the desert.*

I could just make out a road—though I had to look closely to see it. Given all the wind-blown sand, it looked like there was no road at all, only a sea of dust blowing in the wind.

A vehicle was moving down below me—a large vessel, a military carrier, moving through the center of the desert. They looked strong, but isolated.

What could they see from inside, *I wondered?*

They were alone in a sprawling wilderness of sand. And that's when I realized this vehicle was about to be attacked and that everyone inside could be killed.

I have to stop it from happening, *I thought as I saw the vehicle approaching a point where I knew a trap was laid for it.*

You cannot stop it from happening, *a voice inside me said.*

It is already done.

I suddenly knew that earlier that day, young men had come alongside the road to dig a hole in the ground. They had studied the routes of the soldiers and knew their routine. They would come this way, and an Improvised Explosive Device (IED) would hit them right on time. It was a trap they could not see.

I have to stop it, *I thought as I surveyed the surrounding territory.*

I have to warn these soldiers. But there was no help to be found on the road.

The carrier was speeding along, right on time. Suddenly, an explosion sent shockwaves through the air. The vehicle was hit, and it was hit hard.

As the carrier rolled to its side, I could see within it. Several people were jolted.

***This one,** a voice said—then my vision focused in on one man in particular.*

He needs to make it. He is a special one.

I focused on this one soldier pointed out to me. I focused my energy, as if to pray. I could see that he was badly injured. **God be with him and let him make it out alive.**

Then, I woke up. Lying there in the dark, the dream felt so real, as if I were back in Afghanistan and fully awake. I had another sense, too, as if that man needed me at *that very instant*.

I prayed.

God, be with the man in the carrier. Grant him a speedy recovery and long life. Help him to fulfill the mission you have given him. Preserve him and keep him, so that he might protect others from harm. Amen.

Dreams: A Vision of Reality

You may be thinking: I don't have special dreams like this. Or I don't believe that dreams are necessarily from God—if there is one.

Yes, I personally believe these are special dreams which have shown me God's purpose for my life, to protect people in harm's way and to boldly serve those in need.

But here is a bigger, just as important point I want you to consider:

What are dreams, but a vision of the reality we want to see?

Even if you do not have dramatic dreams, I believe everyone is given a vision.

Dreams are thoughts with vision.

They can become especially important when you experience a dark night of the soul.

Working in disaster and war zones will test your assumption that people are ultimately good. You are going to see people harm each other and harm other living things. This might tempt you to think that, in the epic battle between good and evil, evil wins. But you can't let thoughts like this consume you or else you will become unable to focus on your work. That is why you need a vision and a core belief in humanity to keep you going. In addition to recognizing the darkness, you need to seek the light—the light of human kindness and the beauty that comes from within the human spirit—to sustain you. Go ahead, and dream of a better world. It's worth it.

Your very thoughts, even now, help form and shape a vision for how you want to live your life, for how you see the world.

What vision is coming into focus in your life?

How do you want to contribute to the needs you see around you? Like me, you are growing your own garden by the words and actions you take every day. What kind of life are you cultivating?

Living a life of service gives us an opportunity to live in solidarity with others. If we understand people's needs, we can be part of the solution to their plight. For people of faith, it means having solidarity with them in our devotion, not only in the work we do but in spiritual expressions of prayer.

Even if you are not a person who has a certain faith, you can make a difference in the world by what I think of as "being mindful of others" and "having spiritual practices," that is, ways to show your belief in a better world. Here are a few of those acts:

Mindfulness. Be mindful of people in their suffering through moments of silence, meditation, and other forms of artistic expression. When a good friend of mine received a cancer diagnosis, I decided the best way to pray for her would be through praise in celebration of her life, believing that she would recover. I knew that others remained mindful of her condition and offered "good thoughts," "good wishes," and "positive energy." Personally, I felt the urge to declare victory for her, because that was what she needed. She was, indeed, victorious. She has been in remission and free from cancer for five years.

Live boldly. One of the best things you can do to help others is to live boldly, that is, not to accept the status quo or the easy answer to a problem. By believing that change is possible, you will have the fortitude to find solutions that will last. By being bold, you can bring together a diverse team of people to change the community where you live for the better. **Wherever you are, decide to live passionately, not passively.**

Live in solidarity with those who suffer. Even long after leaving people or places, they stay with you. Though you cannot remain in touch with thousands of people in a refugee camp, you can remember their faces and the places where they lived. You can declare a blessing over their life, a sign of hope, a promise to come, and offer encouragement to keep them going when things get hard.

Take part in public services and remembrances. You don't have to belong to a community of faith to provide support to suffering people. Collective expressions of solidarity happen within and outside the community of faith. These expressions really do matter. Not because God needs us, but because people are crying out in pain and, amidst their affliction, we can provide relief by showing them they are not forgotten.

All of us can provide resources and supplies, believing they will make a life-saving difference. We can "speak truth to power" and urge the authorities to work toward policies that will end wars and reduce violence. Advocate for people in need by contacting your local officials and letting them know that you support humanitarian programs that help refugees and disaster affected communities.

Changing the World

Your faith in humanity can give you the power to see the world around you with fresh eyes and the courage needed to shape the course of world events. My experience tells me that **you will rely on your instincts, your core beliefs, and your faith in humanity to complete the work you have to do in the world.**

Go forward in great courage. Living from the core of your being and cultivating a spiritual life can help you know what to do next. Even the notional ideas you have, the things that randomly come to mind, can be guiding forces of divine intervention. I have had too many spiritual encounters to deny the power of God. You can be part of changing the world by doing your part and having faith that when circumstances are beyond your control, the world is in divine hands and is a good place to be.

9

USING YOUR POWER

"True civilization is where every man gives to every other every right he claims for himself."

Robert Ingersoll

When I see a problem, I want to fix it. But some problems are harder to fix than others. Remember when I told you that the root causes of humanitarian problems are hard to address? One of the most difficult challenges is when national governments fail to respond to the needs of their people. Good governance is key to helping people recover from conflict and disaster.

Therein lies the issue.

Every government has its constituency, the people to whom it responds. In some countries, the government represents a particular state or territory. In other countries, the government can represent a powerful family or ethnic group. These groups can wield power over other groups in tyrannical ways, causing some people to be safe while others are harmed, making some people wealthy while others live in poverty. Abuses of power abound when a state or government uses power as a way to monopolize wealth rather than distributing shared resources in the form of goods and services to the people.

Although governments have a responsibility to provide basic administrative and public services to their people, this responsibility is often abdicated in order to award huge benefits to a small group of elites. Many conflicts in the world today remain unresolved because of this imbalance of power between an elite group of politicians or military leaders and the citizenry.

After the Rwandan genocide and ethnic cleansing in the Balkans, the United Nations emphasized that governments have a primary responsibility to protect their citizens, and the international community has a right to respond when governments fail to protect their people. Oftentimes, humanitarian agencies step in where there is an absence of a responsible governing authority.

Governance and Disasters

When a disaster strikes or war breaks out, aid can be diverted to certain locations in favor of a particular group of people, while aid is withheld from other areas. Sometimes governments, in an effort to reassure people that everything is under control, declare that the situation is better than the reality.

In a humanitarian emergency, many people die from preventable causes that could have been resolved by government authorities. Therefore, a lack of leadership is one of the biggest gaps in humanitarian crises to fix problems. These problems often have to be addressed at the political level. When national authorities are unable or unwilling to protect people from violence or provide proper assistance to meet people's needs, the international community steps up and tries to help. Even if national leaders are absent, indecisive, or corrupt, humanitarian agencies will work to identify local, community, and municipal authorities who can make decisions about priorities for the relief effort. Sometimes, there are no government officials or offices to coordinate within the area of need. Working with affected populations and ensuring that relief is based on their priorities becomes especially important under these circumstances.

In a democracy, all people are valuable because they have the power to vote their representatives into office. Yet, powerful interest groups try to sway elected leaders to focus on issues or problems affecting people with certain financial interests at the expense of decisions that improve the well-being of all people. Even in a country as powerful as the United States, this has led to the neglect of poor communities, which suffer more than others when a disaster strikes.

For example, when Hurricane Katrina struck the Gulf Coast of Louisiana, it was a watershed moment for the United States emergency response system and a turning point in my humanitarian career. When the storm hit, I was in Washington, D.C. working as the Director of Government Relations for the U.S. Committee for Refugees and Immigrants. The focus of my job was advocating for refugees with the U.S. Congress and the Executive Branch. I had recently returned to the U.S. from working with the United Nations in Afghanistan.

Because of my experience in Afghanistan, I quickly became friends with officials working on homeland security. I had done some charitable volunteer work in the United States, but responding to Hurricane Katrina was the first major emergency I responded to in my home country. The experience forever changed my view on what it means to be an American. I realized that meeting the needs of people affected by disaster in the United States is a civic duty. It is the very least we can do for our neighbors who work hard and pay taxes to the government.

Man-Made Disaster

Hurricane Katrina was a natural disaster, but it was also a man-made disaster because government officials at multiple levels abdicated their responsibility to protect people from harm. First, the Mayor of New Orleans failed to issue a mandatory evacuation order requiring people to leave the area. This was the first step to getting people out of harm's way before the storm hit. The Mayor did not know how devastating the storm would, in fact, become. He also thought it was logistically impossible to evacuate everyone in such a short period of time. He was wrong.

Second, after the storm hit, state officials did not use all the resources at their disposal to help those affected. State agencies that were familiar with the needs of the population, such as the Department of Health and Human Services, were closed. As state officials argued for more resources from federal officials, this created unnecessary gaps in services.

Third, federal officials were woefully unprepared to offer the city or the state the amount of help it needed. The Federal Emergency Management Agency (FEMA) put up obstacles to helping people by issuing more rules and "red tape" than relief items. This tied up the effort in bureaucratic procedures, keeping aid from reaching people.

When government leaders came together, they made bad choices about how to help. They placed families in temporary trailers and gave them cash vouchers (in areas where supplies were limited) instead of putting them in rental housing in safe locations where they could go to work, buy supplies, and resume their normal lives. Having so many officials with varying levels of authority all along the process of making decisions for the relief effort meant that each person at every level had to choose the best interest of those affected over political expediency in order to get it right.

This is why they failed.

We Can Do Better

Seeing these decisions play out poorly on the ground, I was shocked that the United States did not do better for the people of New Orleans. Humanitarian aid is supposed to be about the needs of the people, as determined by sound assessments. Instead, officials were busy looking out for their own interests. Leaders made decisions based on their own perception of what was happening, with limited information or knowledge of the situation on the ground. Officials gave interviews to the press indicating they were doing a great job when the situation was, in fact, out of control.

The storm and its horrific aftermath showed me that government institutions which should have protected the people were not doing the job. It would take outside advocates and organizations to show the government what was really happening and to offer a way forward.

When I returned to Washington, D.C. from New Orleans, I worked with a coalition of agencies on a new plan for Louisiana. We recommended resettling people outside the affected area, placing them in rental housing where adults could work and earn the money they needed to rebuild. The plan would have taken every family out of mass shelter in a matter of weeks, which was an important step in the recovery process. The White House reviewed and rejected the plan as being too costly. One official said he did not want to help people who didn't vote for his political party. Eventually, the government permitted a foreign country to grant funds to agencies willing to relocate people. Yet, many evacuees spent months in mass shelters, sleeping on cots, waiting in long lines for food, not knowing when they could go home.

Many years afterward, I believed that having a better government was the only way to change the system. I wanted to be part of making things better, to be in a position of power so I could make decisions that save lives.

Eventually, as I thought back on my work, I realized that I did have the power to change lives, just as I am, without an important position. Each thing I did for any one person led me to help an even greater number of people. That's because each person I met took me down a path of deeper understanding so that I could respond to greater challenges in the road ahead. I was showing leadership every time I worked to resolve problems on behalf of people in need.

You also have the power to address the problems you see in the world. You need to learn how to use that power wisely by preparing yourself and being willing to step up to leadership when the time comes.

I had to learn that even when I was not in a powerful position, I could make a difference by summoning the personal courage to speak up for those in need. When faced with political authorities that were not responsive to the needs of the people, I learned that I had the power to act by advocating on people's behalf. It wasn't necessary to have the right position or job title. I already had the power. I had a strong sense of civic duty and moral courage to speak up for people who lost everything.

I understood then that what it takes for any of us to make a difference, great or small, is the willingness to step up to leadership, however you can. You do not need to be in a position of power to help people. You can be a good friend, a good neighbor, by living out your civic duty every day.

As an American, I felt deeply convicted that the country could do better for disaster-affected people in our own back yard. I stepped up to the plate by assessing people's needs and offering real solutions to relieve their suffering. I used whatever individual courage I had to speak up for the people.

Being a leader is about being willing to take on obligations and responsibilities.

It's not about sitting on the sidelines and blaming someone else when something bad happens. A real leader runs toward a problem and doesn't stop working until a solution is found. I learned this by seeing how powerful leaders get things done in Washington.

Your Personal Power

When I worked in the Senate, I carefully observed my boss, then Senator Olympia J. Snowe of Maine. I looked at the way she carried herself. She knew she had the authority of being an elected official, but she used her power selectively, applying pressure on key votes where she wanted to see changes in policy, such as advancing women's access to health care. By watching her careful judgement, I came up with three rules about how to apply personal power:

1. Claim responsibility
2. Own your authority
3. Have self-respect

The easiest thing to do when you see a problem is blame someone else. Choosing to claim personal responsibility for the problem automatically places you in the driver's seat toward finding a solution. It means you are willing to step up and be a leader.

Senator Snowe took responsibility for the well-being of the country and my home state of Maine. Claiming this responsibility was something she could reasonably do by virtue of her office. While working for her, this also helped me carry out my civic duty by improving the responsiveness of the government to the people every day.

The Senator was a powerful, elected official. After being sworn in, she received the title of *The Honorable Senator from Maine*, an office with tall ceilings, State and Senate seals, and a budget for a staff to carry out her plans. But those things alone did not make her powerful. She owned the authority she was given by the way she carried herself. She took it upon herself to exercise that authority in limited ways so that every time she wanted to achieve something, she succeeded. She also had an enduring respect for herself and her office so that no one could diminish her or take anything away from her.

By working for the Senator, I saw the difference between power that is bestowed by a position and *power that comes from within*. **I learned that anyone could have power if they used it correctly.**

Chuck

Even before I had "a real job," I learned that I had the power to change a person's life. In high school, I played soccer until the summer of my senior year, when the lead striker on our team accidentally broke my leg. She struck a blow to my femur bone, which meant that I would be sitting on the bench my final year of school.

After sitting on the bench for a while, I decided to do something better with my time. I went to the United Way to ask where volunteers were needed most in my community. They told me there was a great need for adult literacy volunteers, which meant teaching grown-ups how to read. I was surprised to learn that seven percent of adults in Maine, a few hundred thousand people, could not read or write.

After several weeks of training on how to teach adult learners, I was ready to meet with clients. In the evenings, I would go back to school to work with clients who were looking for help with reading.

Most of my clients were adult men. One man, Chuck, was a construction worker. He came in each night in a t-shirt and blue jeans, wearing utility boots. The first night I met him, he told me he dropped out of school in the 8th grade to help his family pay the bills. He didn't have a high school diploma, so he could only do certain jobs, but he was still a hard worker. Chuck was tall and physically strong. You would never know talking with him, carrying on an intelligent conversation, that he couldn't read.

I asked him, "What makes you want to read now?"

A smile spread across his face. "I became a father," he said. "I want to read to my baby girl."

He took out his wallet and showed me her picture.

"She's still small," I said.

He replied, "She doesn't know that I can't read now, but I'm going to learn before she finds out."

Then I asked him how he managed to go this long without reading. He was already in his 30s. "There are all kinds of ways," he said, "of asking people to read things for you."

By the time I finished my senior year, Chuck was reading to his little girl. Once I got to college, I was too busy to continue serving as a literacy volunteer.

I had learned, however, that *even when faced with your own limitations, you can always help someone else.* Even that little bit of help you give can change a life—and perhaps more than one. The lesson learned with Chuck would later come back to me.

Call from the White House

Sometimes circumstances ask you to step up to civic leadership on a grander scale.

At the break of dawn, Hurricane Katrina made landfall in Louisiana. The epic Category 4 hurricane had sustained winds of 145 miles per hour. When the eye of the storm passed right over New Orleans, local, state, and federal officials were still scrambling, arguing about whether mandatory evacuations were necessary.

Then the levees, which held back water from flooding the city, broke. **All hell broke loose on the second day** as tens of thousands of people from the Lower 9th Ward went toward the Superdome seeking shelter.

Mystified by the ensuing chaos, I saw the storm hit New Orleans while watching the news from the comfort of my living room. Local television crews outside the large sports arena covered the horrific scene outside; elderly people slumped over in wheelchairs had passed out and died, and people were sleeping outside beside the dead bodies. Adults were begging for water; babies were crying for food. National Guard officers stood by, keeping watch over the building.

I could barely stand to watch the situation play out before me on the news. When I went into work the next day, my boss called me to her office.

"I just received a call from the White House," she said. *"They asked for you by name, Sarah.* They want you to go down there as soon as possible. They're getting a lot of different reports. They need an independent assessment of the needs. They want a plan for what to do with all the displaced people."

At that moment, I wondered, *who asked for me by name?* I had contact with government officials about Afghanistan and Africa, but not about Louisiana. I couldn't figure it out, but I was *ready to go.*

Hurricane Katrina: A Catastrophic Crisis

I arrived in Baton Rouge with a colleague who worked with the U.S. military in Iraq and would help us link up with the military side of the response.

Immediately, we learned that drinking water was in short supply and had to be rationed. Water needed to be boiled to be sure it wasn't contaminated by the flood waters. We took showers from a bucket, with a cup to pour water over our heads as if we were in a remote village.

When we drove around Baton Rouge the next morning, the situation was catastrophic. Families of six slept in cars in vacant lots. Barely clad men walked the streets. When people saw us assessing conditions with clipboards in hand, they came up to us, naked, asking,

"Where can we get some clothes?"

The Red Cross shelters were full. The largest one was next to a casino, the only open business other than a dive bar on the other side of town that decided, with the influx of people, to start serving food. When we stopped there for chicken and biscuits, crowds of hungry people came up to us, begging,

"Where can we find food?"

Even after working in a war zone, I was overwhelmed by the chaos. My next inclination was to go to the command center, which was set up by the Army. My colleague had military identification, and I had an ID badge from my NGO office. We were as official as we could be, and representatives from the federal government were expecting us. We had appointments.

The lesson to be learned from a disaster situation like this is: you can't rely on media reports to understand the nature of the problem. You have to do your own reconnaissance. Gather firsthand information. Conduct a needs assessment. Let your findings guide the response so you can appropriately address the need. Most importantly, don't assume that things will go according to plan. Expect complications.

Water Needs

Once we got inside the command center, the badges didn't matter. We went from division to division. Everyone was so busy managing the crisis, they had no time for us. To my surprise, no one was focused on helping the people right outside the doors. Inside the government, officials were focused on preventing the collapse of critical infrastructure rather than on people's immediate need for survival.

Officials asked us to go to a Disaster Recovery Center opening in the morning. It was meant to be a one-stop shop for people to make claims for assistance with the Federal Emergency Management Agency (FEMA). When we arrived first thing the next day, hours before the center opened, 500 people were already lined up outside. The elderly women and the babies were clearly dehydrated, passing out in line. If they didn't get water immediately, they would soon need medical attention.

We made several calls describing the situation and asked to see what kind of help was staged inside the recovery center. We asked, "Is there enough water inside for the 500 people waiting in line?" When someone from headquarters came to unlock the door, we gasped. There were no supplies inside. No water, no food, no computers to register people or account for their needs. *The people were waiting in line for nothing, for help that would never come.*

We went back to the command center and told the Army Corps of Engineers about the severe need for water. Behind their desks were thousands of bottles of water stacked high along the walls, right up to the ceiling. I asked them if they would bring water to the recovery center:

"Hundreds of desperate people are in line, and they are severely dehydrated."

They told me "No," the supplies were for *them*, the Army. They wouldn't give the people any of their own supply. Hundreds of cases of water were right there in front of me, and less than a mile away people were passing out from dehydration, but we couldn't take the water to them. I asked the engineers at the desk:

"Can you tell me: what exactly is your priority?" I asked them.

One said, "Ma'am, we are trying to repair the infrastructure so more levees don't break. There are several other dams about to breech that will make the situation worse if we don't fix it now. You can't take our supplies. *Go to the churches around town—ask them for water.*"

But the levees had broken only two days before. Flood water was everywhere, even in the house where we were staying. We could see the flood lines up to our shoulders on the wall. The lines of mold were visible in every room of the house. The smell of mold permeated everything. The chance that the local water supply was contaminated was high.

How were the churches, or any other local source, supposed to supply clean drinking water? There was no water to be found.

No matter; we realized that we had to reach out for any resources possible, anywhere we could find them. We ourselves had to be resourceful. We had already wasted precious hours trying to get supplies. Time was of the essence. This was an emergency.

Relief at Last

We went to the churches. Church volunteers got on the phone with the congregations. Details went out about how much water was needed and where the recovery center was located. Seeing that the churches were acting fast to help, we went back to check on the situation.

When the women at the Disaster Recovery Center saw us coming back empty handed, they got angry. They thought we were in charge. Several large women formed a circle around us, yelling aggressively.

"Where is the help? Where is the help?"

They started poking their fingers at us, and all we could do was move away, defensively, and say apologetically, "It's coming."

Within minutes, private security forces descended upon the center. Young men with loaded weapons and dark sunglasses arrived looking like they jumped out of a plane from the Iraq War. The armed guards pointed their weapons at the women. The situation was tense.

"Stand down," I told the armed guards. Using my hand, I gave them a waving motion to turn their guns away. "These women are tired and thirsty. They have a right to be upset."

My colleague assured the women, *"Help is coming."* It sounded like a wish or a prayer. Within minutes, church volunteers started arriving with cases of water. I thanked God. The women, children, and elderly cried tears of relief. It was their first drink of water in days.

I stood there, shocked that our colleagues at the command center had organized a private security detail *for us* rather than getting water to our fellow Americans.

How was it possible to be so efficient for security yet so ineffective for the people? What kind of disaster response system had we built as a country if it couldn't put people first?

That night, we checked on the Red Cross shelters. They were all full. As I mentioned before, the largest one was next to a casino. It was a sight to see at night, an awkward dichotomy. People in the shelters would go outside to smoke or talk in private, while private security contractors gambled away their earnings next door. The contractors were making upwards of $10,000 a month to provide security for the "relief effort."

Forever after, I would always remember that disaster scenes can present gross inequalities within society. I would remember, too, that you can't let the injustice staring you in the face drag you down, however tempting it might be to get angry. Nonetheless, you can't let the injustice go either. You have to let it change your approach so you can tackle the underlying causes of the problem. At that moment, I embraced the call to work toward systemic changes that would make people less vulnerable in my home country.

Evacuee Camps in Arkansas

In the meantime, evacuees were being moved from the Superdome in New Orleans to the Astrodome in Houston, Texas. That, too, became overcrowded. Looking for solutions, officials began dispersing evacuees to other states.

When Arkansas offered to receive evacuees from Louisiana, the Governor's office called my organization. Could we help them figure out what to do next? I got on a plane to Little Rock to offer our support.

Officials in the state capital decided to place evacuees in church camps, where there was an excess of shelter and willing volunteers in the community. They asked if I would go visit the camps that received large numbers of people.

When I got to the first camp, I met with the church leaders. They were used to being camp counselors for young people, but they had never housed adults in the facility before. I asked them to describe the intake process for me.

They told me, "We assigned a certain number of people to each cabin, put up a notice about the meal schedule, showed them where the computers are so they can track their claim forms for federal assistance, and, well, that's about it. Now people stay in their cabins."

I noticed that everyone running the camp was white, and all the evacuees were black. Without pointing out the clear racial differences, I asked them if they talked to the evacuees since they arrived to see how they were doing. "No," they said. They only spoke with the evacuees if someone made a special request.

I began walking around, going to each cabin to conduct an initial needs assessment. I was alarmed to find children with adults who were unrelated to them. Some of the children had not seen a family member since the storm. I also identified men whose most recent residence was a state prison. People were mixed together who should have been separated and referred to social services.

By the time I got back to the camp cafeteria, I sensed that a man was following me. When I turned around and asked if I could help him, he asked me if I would look at his federal claim forms. I willingly said, "Yes." I stood beside him as we went through each question:

Do you own a home?

"No."

Do you rent a residence?

"Yes, but it was washed out by the storm."

Do you have flood insurance?

"No."

What is your annual income?

"I don't know. I get cash payments at the crawfish processing plant."

What bank do you use?

"I don't have a bank account."

Have you ever had a bank account?

"No," he replied. Then, it dawned on me to ask,

"Can you read this form?"

"No," he said, looking down at his feet.

I told him we had better sit down. Within minutes, a line of another 200 evacuees formed around us with their paperwork in hand. None of them had made claims for assistance because they could not read or understand the forms.

The Right Kind of Help

At the end of the day, I explained to the manager of the church camp that a formal needs assessment should be done to make sure that each person was accounted for and referred to the appropriate services. I explained that they had to immediately separate unaccompanied children from unrelated adults and call social services about reuniting the children with a family member.

I also told the staff that everyone needed help with reading. They should speak with each person individually to help them complete the federal registration form for assistance. The manager of the camp said, *"Well, that explains it. We had no idea why they weren't using the computers to fill out their forms online. We had no idea they can't read."*

Not only couldn't the people read, but as I helped them fill out their forms, I realized that most of them never owned anything (not a house or a car), they did not carry any insurance (flood or personal), and many people had never had a bank account. They had worked in the cash economy their whole lives.

When you are doing relief work, always remember some people may not have the skills—like computer savvy or even the ability to read—that you and I take for granted. Find out how to help in the most basic manner because that is often what's needed.

A Better America

When I returned to Washington, I wrote a report about the situation. The bottom line was that New Orleans was still a mess. The only way for people to return to normalcy was to move them away from the disaster zone.

The big-picture solution for evacuees was to stage people outside the disaster zone but with targeted assistance that would allow them to start working as soon as possible. Evacuees needed financial liquidity; they needed to earn cash so they could move out of temporary shelter and find decent housing. The children needed to be reunited with relatives and live in places where schools were open. New Orleans was still a mess.

However, government officials were skeptical about relocating communities. They decided to house people in trailers and give them cash vouchers. But no stores were open to buy anything from, except for pawn shops. Government officials could not understand why an evacuee who needed food and shelter would spend money on jewelry and expensive sneakers. The disaster zone did not have functional markets where people could buy the right supplies, and the population was not used to having large cash disbursements at their disposal. Instead of large payments, I argued for rent and transportation vouchers so people could find a place to go where they could resume their normal lives.

Although my agency and other organizations presented a viable plan to the government, White House officials rejected it on the basis that it was "too expensive." One official told us, *These are not our people. They will never pay us back,"* inferring that poor black people from Louisiana were not a good return on investment. I tried to explain that every citizen mattered, regardless of their race or financial position. In that moment, I knew that my work would never be the same. I had to do more.

If we do not care for our people, who will we become as a country?

Even within the United States, in the event of a major crisis, the responsibility to protect people from harm is a challenge. Disasters can stir up harsh inequalities between those in need and the very people charged with protecting the nation. As a humanitarian, when you are faced with these perplexing issues, you have to stay the course, holding firm to the principle that people are more important than politics. This may require digging deep within yourself and working against the odds to accomplish your mission. Ultimately, you might have to adjust the scope of your calling.

Getting Political

At that point, I decided it was time to get involved in politics. The United States needed a government that took responsibility for its citizens and cared for the needs of all its people regardless of race, economic status, or their voting record. Inspired by the upcoming election, I changed jobs to work on presidential campaigns.

For the next two years, I advised international organizations on outreach to the presidential candidates and their foreign policy circles. I spent time in the early caucus and primary states of Iowa and New Hampshire, hosting town halls on humanitarian issues. Driving through the corn fields of Iowa, I thought about Eleanor Roosevelt, the former First Lady who brought nations together to sign the Universal Declaration of Human Rights at the United Nations. I thought about her famous quote:

*"You gain strength, courage, and confidence by every experience in which you really stop to look fear in the face. **You must do the thing you think you cannot do.**"*
Eleanor Roosevelt

I wanted to elect a new government, a government *for the people* that stood up to the ideals of our founders who believed that all men and women were created equal: the poor woman, the immigrant child, the black man, and those who could not read.

Being a literacy volunteer in high school helped me teach one man to read. But learning how illiterate people function in society allowed me to reach out to hundreds of confused evacuees who did not know how to access help.

After a disaster, people need more than short-term relief. They also need education and economic opportunities to lift them out of poverty over the long haul. If the government did not take responsibility for people who were marginalized, we would not be living up to our ideals as a nation. It was time for new leadership in America that reflected the hope and aspirations of all people.

Like me, you can probably identify problems within your home community that are too big for any one person or agency to solve. The root cause of these problems may involve entrenched racial, social, and economic inequalities. When people in power are not addressing the problems you see, there are a number of ways you can use your personal power to make a difference.

Step up to Leadership

Be willing to step up to leadership. You are powerful every time you speak up for others, you refuse to accept the status quo, and you try to make a difference. Although some people may wonder: who does this person think she is? Remember, no one has become a leader by staying in the background and being quiet.

Being a leader means accepting responsibility, being willing to address problems head on, and claiming the authority to offer solutions. This authority can come from civic duty and a sense of citizenship, and it can come from a specific role or position you have earned by virtue of your education and experience.

Get Involved

Volunteering with a local nonprofit or social service provider is a great way to see what is happening right in your community.

Ask the United Way about which nonprofits need the most support. If there is a Red Cross chapter in your area, become a disaster response volunteer. Get involved with your neighborhood civic association and take care of your neighbors.

Advocate for Change

Stay informed of policy issues affecting your city and state, as well as national and world events. **Vote.** Organize your friends and neighbors to vote. Organize meetings with your elected officials about issues you care about, including disaster response. Apply to work in the local, state, or federal government. Consider running for office yourself.

Be willing to work with people who may not share your perspective or political opinions. Be collaborative and reach out to community groups that can work on problems together. These could be bipartisan policy coalitions or inter-faith working groups addressing discrimination and other forms of violence within your community.

Become Time-Wise

Even if you do not have a lot of money to give, you have something more important to offer—your time. Consider how you spend your time in the evenings and weekends. Are there things you could be doing with your free time to make a difference?

Give Whenever Possible

If you are fortunate to have the financial resources to give money, consider giving unrestricted donations. Organizations need cash to allocate resources where the need is greatest. Plan out your giving through regular, monthly, or annual contributions and recurring payments.

Make annual contributions during tax season. Engage your family in decisions about giving.

Organize Those Around You

Mobilizing people to come together around a particular cause or issue is a powerful way to multiply your impact. If you volunteer with or donate to one organization, encourage that group to partner with other organizations in the community. Plan joint events and meetings that increase the number of people who are working to address the same problem.

When you see coverage of a foreign crisis on the news, it is understandable to feel removed, since the situation is so far away. Despite the distance, there are ways you can live in solidarity with those who are suffering. But when a crisis strikes your local community, you can make a difference by being prepared to respond.

The great needs we see in the world today are not so far away. There are needs right in your own back yard. Everywhere around you, there are people in need for whom you could be a lifeline. Don't be a bystander. Get involved in your community.

In the United States, we have a shared responsibility for one another. It is our civic duty to care for our fellow man, woman, and child. The belief that we are to look out for each other, no matter where we come from, makes us unique. The great seal of the United States established by an Act of Congress in 1782 states, in Latin:

E pluribus unum. **(Out of many, we are one.)**

We must strive to live up to this ideal. We cannot afford to lose our sense of civic duty that compels us to work for the common good. For it is enshrined in the Declaration of Independence that:

"All men are created equal, they are endowed by their Creator with certain unalienable rights. Among these are Life, Liberty, and the Pursuit of Happiness."

For those who are born American citizens, this comes with significant individual rights to determine the course of our own future.

How, then, can we hope for anything less for our fellow human beings?

I hope this chapter has shown you that each and every one of us—whether you live in the United States or a country plagued by war—has a critical role to play in helping people in need.

At one point, we will each be called to respond to the challenges of our time: environmental degradation, water shortages, disease, information warfare, and migration. Be ready to respond. Be willing to step up to leadership.

As you work to help others, you will be strengthened by individual purpose and our collective resolve to make the world a better place. Let us live up to the power of our ideals and leave no one behind.

10

A DARK NIGHT

"In a real dark night of the soul, it is always 3 a.m."
F. Scott Fitzgerald

I have been trained to recognize fear in a person's eyes. I can see danger ahead from miles away and discern patterns of violence in distant places. This is what keeping an eye out for the needs of others will develop in you. Each one of us has the power of observation.

When you work with people in crisis, sometimes you see too much. Human rights advocates call this "bearing witness." Sometimes what you see leads to sensory overload and is simply too much to bear.

In this chapter, I want to discuss how you develop the power of observation to acutely perceive needs as well as what happens when what you observe weighs too heavily on your heart and mind.

What do you do when exposure to sickness, death, and violence overwhelms you? Like so many helpers, I have lived through a few dark nights.

Burning the Dead

By the time I arrived in the capital of Haiti, Port au Prince, they were already burning the dead. My driver handed me a face mask. "Put this on," he said. "It will keep you from inhaling the smoke—and the smell."

Are there any words to describe the smell of burning flesh?

The earth swallowed the lives of its people. The 7.0 Richter scale earthquake was no match for Haiti's feeble infrastructure. Everything around the epicenter of the quake, the entire capital city, had collapsed.

I looked out the window. Men carrying torches set fire to unclaimed bodies by the side of the road. **Hundreds of men, women, and children were set ablaze** like wood to be burned.

The bodies had been left by the road, discarded. In the chaos following the quake, many people could not find their loved ones, dead or alive. The corpses had become a public health risk, as their smell and the inevitable arrival of wild creatures wanting to eat them had become too much of a terrifying spectacle for those who survived.

Elsewhere, cranes had been called in to collect the bodies and bury them in mass graves. When they stopped counting, officials estimated 300,000 people died that day.

As my eyes tried to adjust to the horror of burning flesh around me, I couldn't help but think: that body is someone's mother, someone's child, someone's friend.

Surely someone would like to know where they were, if they were okay or not. Now, they were completely unidentifiable. These bodies would be represented by names on a long list of the people declared missing, then assumed gone, and eventually pronounced dead.

That night, when I arrived at my base, *the songs of those who survived filled the night sky. Hundreds of survivors sang songs throughout the night*—songs of lament for those who had passed and songs of praise for those whose lives were spared.

In between the singing, there was audible sobbing, as countless tears were shed. The collective cry of a people filled the night sky. It was 2010, and Haiti was once again in crisis.

Bearing Witness

As a humanitarian, you are trained to focus your energy on *what you can do to save lives.* In an emergency, there is no time to count the lives that have been lost. The focus is on saving as many lives as possible. A core task of emergency response is conducting a needs assessment; this involves gathering detailed information about how people have been affected by a crisis and how to assist them in order of priority.

Most assessments focus on gaps in access to basic needs, such as food and shelter, so that agencies can determine how much aid is needed. In addition to basic survival needs, some assessments include damage to homes and infrastructure.

As a protection specialist, my assessments focused on determining whether people were safe from harm, whether they feared for their lives, and whether they were deprived of liberty, freedom of movement, and other basic human needs. This included identifying social vulnerabilities of particular groups of people, such as female-headed households, unaccompanied children, and elderly people without family.

The challenge of conducting these assessments is that the needs are always greater than the response. Often times, there is insufficient funding to provide for all the people who need help, and political will to address the source of the crisis is also lacking. Humanitarians have to prioritize who to help, which involves making tough choices and tradeoffs.

Aid workers design programs within their budget realities with the resources they have been given. This often leads to the feeling that what you are doing is not enough. During the tsunami response in southern Thailand, I called my boss to tell her, **"I don't think we're doing enough."** She told me to focus on what we were doing and start from there.

This is how overwhelming feelings can take hold of you.

Tsunami Response

When a tsunami hit southern Thailand in 2004, nearly 230,000 people died. The massive wave of water devastated the resort town of Phuket. Unbeknown to many, a large number of migrants from neighboring Myanmar worked in the area. The country of Myanmar is also known as 'Burma,' but the name was officially changed to Myanmar in 1989 when a military junta took over the government.

Less than 48 hours after the wave hit, my office received distress calls from migrants saying they were unable to send their dead home. The leaders of migrant community groups called our office crying, saying the situation was too dangerous. "The junta in Myanmar will desecrate their bodies. Please, come help us," they said.

My boss sent me to southern Thailand and to the Thai-Myanmar border to meet with local partner organizations. We received funding from the Government of Switzerland to help migrant children whose parents had perished in the storm. Many newly orphaned children were living alone in the migrant labor camps. My organization offered them a safe place to play that included day care, education, clean water, and access to medical care. We also worked to address their problems with the Thai government, including repatriating the remains of those who died in the storm.

Our educational program brought children from the migrant labor camps to a day care several times a week. Some of the children we cared for were being abused. I found out because one little girl, Mi, was always disappearing from the group.

Once you focus in on a single person and their plight, emotions can become more difficult to keep out of your work. You want to help that one person, to change their circumstances. Sometimes you cannot save them from violence.

Little Mi

Something strange was going on with Little Mi, an adorable 5-year-old girl with pigtails on either side of her head and a missing front tooth. She kept disappearing from the other children. When I noticed this, I asked the other counselors about her. After the tsunami, Mi's parents were still alive, but her father was a fisherman who went out to sea each day. Her mother sold fish at the market. During the day, she was left alone in a large slum for migrant workers.

I had been in the migrant labor camps. They were hidden behind five-star hotels and convenience stores. People were piled on top of one another, on top of garbage. The conditions were abhorrent, some of the worst I had ever seen.

Behind one convenience store, people lived on top of tons of waste. Makeshift shelters were propped up on top of garbage, with bamboo stakes and sheeting providing shelter for hundreds of migrants. The workers had to pay the owner of the store "rent" to live there and keep the police away so the migrant workers would not be deported to Myanmar. The store also sold dirty water to the workers for drinking, cooking, and bathing. This caused numerous skin problems and diseases within the community.

As I walked on top of the garbage, men, women, and children would show me the lesions on their skin. I documented the horrific condition in which they lived by taking pictures and notes. But nothing could document my disgust that human beings would allow other people to live this way.

This is an example of the compounded and complex situations in which you may find yourself. Assessing and sorting out which situations you can reasonably manage is one thing. Handling the personal impact of what you witness is also an important task, and one you have to plan for—no one likes to see people suffer day after day. Yet, out in the field, in real life conditions, what you see requires you to manage your personal reaction so you don't become paralyzed. **You are there to find a way to help, and you must complete your mission.**

Another labor camp was located behind a five-star hotel. This camp was made up of raggedy shacks housing thousands of workers who were rebuilding the resorts. In the middle of the camp, a large square trough provided the only source of water for the camp. Construction materials contaminated the water where everyone bathed. There were no services in the camp for migrants injured on the job. I met men with serious electrical wounds, including one man whose hand was nearly cut off. When I offered to take him to the hospital, he refused. He did not want to be identified as an illegal immigrant and risk being deported. He preferred to lose his hand. He had another one.

Mi lived in a labor camp like this, teeming with people coming and going to different jobs. People living there had two goals: making money and not being detected by the police so they wouldn't be returned to Myanmar. The care and protection of children was an afterthought.

In every migrant camp we visited, the children would follow us around. Many of them knew the social workers in our day care program, who were from the local community. They would stop us every few minutes and ask if we were taking them out to play. When we explained "not today," they would cry. Then, they would tell us, "I want to play every day." Their desire to simply be children and to live in a place where they could play tugged at my heart.

To get to the bottom of what was happening to Mi, I shadowed her play time, observing her closely. Sure enough, one minute she was running around with her friends, and the next moment, she was gone. Since I was following her closely, I could see what she was doing. She was hiding.

She hid under a chair, crouching low with her arms wrapped tightly around her legs and her head down. She was trying to make herself smaller so no one would see her. I got down on her level. On my hands and knees, peering under the chair, I asked,

"Mi, why are you hiding? Don't you want to play with your friends?"

"The men will get me. They are coming for me."

"Not here," I told her. *"Here, you are in a safe place. Come out now and go play with your friends. See, they are waiting for you."*

I slowly coaxed her out from under the chair, and she returned to play. Afterward, my team discussed what more we could do. I decided to increase the number of days children could play in the program, which meant hiring more staff and increasing the program budget. We also scheduled "home visits" for our social workers to check-in on the children regularly.

When it was time for me to leave, I could not stop thinking about little Mi. Although I did what I could, it didn't seem like it was enough. She could still be taken at night. We suspected that the men taking her were police officers, and there was no accountability for the abuse of migrant children. However, we could raise the protection of refugee and migrant children by speaking with Thai authorities, encouraging them to adopt policies allowing foreign children to go to school and to strengthen social services for all children, regardless of their national origin.

I could not stay in the south to resolve all the issues I found there. My organization would continue advocating for their needs with government officials, but I had to move on to the border, where another 400,000 people from Burma lived in refugee camps. We had a longstanding relationship with refugee organizations that had been operating on the Thai-Myanmar border for decades.

Thai-Myanmar Border

When I first arrived on the border of Thailand and Myanmar, the leaders of a local organization assisting refugees welcomed me. They gave me an overview of their programs as we walked to various locations where they had health and educational programs for refugees.

This gave me an overview of the situation. A broad overview is necessary to help you understand the scope of a problem.

Now it was time to go deeper, into the details of how people were being forced to live. This would help focus me in on specific situations in which I might be able to intervene.

When they took me to the safe house for women, no one greeted us at the door. Inside, it was dimly lit. Women sat together in a circle, sewing quietly. It was not your usual gathering of women. They were not talkative, and I didn't force a conversation. I felt the solemn sadness of what they experienced, and we gave them the privacy they needed.

Everywhere we went, there were specific needs to address. The community was struggling to pay for drugs to address the growing number of refugees who had contracted the HIV/AIDS virus. Antiretroviral (ARV) drugs were available in Thailand, but they cost too much money to pay for everyone who needed them. Community organizations were also divided about whether they should pay for the drugs—among other priorities—and how to prevent people from contracting the disease. With support from United Nations agencies, I was able to negotiate a better price for bulk rates of HIV medication at the local clinics so that any refugee who contracted the disease would have access to life-saving medication.

Tragedy Amidst Humor

On my last night at the border, the community came together to put on a theatrical show. A young man wearing a blonde wig played me, carrying out skits about my desire to help his people. The community had been watching me closely the whole week. Somehow this young Asian man was able to capture my words and mannerisms, causing the entire audience to roar in laughter. I also cracked up at the sight of it, watching a parody about my character in the Burmese language.

But the jovial nature of the play was mostly lost on me because *I was carefully observing another young man in the audience.* I had not seen him before, and I could not tell his age. He was older than a child, but his body was so emaciated, he looked more like a small animal rather than a human being. I wondered why community leaders had not brought him to my attention. We went over all the critical cases of HIV, and this was the most acute case of AIDS that I had ever seen.

As the boy with the blonde wig danced on stage, and the audience erupted with laughter about foreigners who tried to help, it dawned on me. *This other young man in the audience was not going to make it.* No amount of anti-retroviral drugs or other health interventions would save his life. It was too late. He was going to die.

This reality of living among the dying, of laughing alongside tragedy, represents the dichotomy of humanitarian work. Among the highlights of saving lives, there are many other people whom you cannot save. Yet, life goes on.

It is hard to accept that you cannot fix every problem you see in the field, but this is an important part of maturing in the work. There are real obstacles to reaching people in time and to preventing bad things from happening to people. There are people who aren't going to make it—who are going to die. Some of those people might be your close friends and colleagues.

Caring for Your Mental Health

When I returned home from Thailand, my agency worked to put pressure on the government to offer stronger protections for migrants affected by the tsunami. This included providing basic services such as education and health care to people from Myanmar working in fishing and construction, industries that were vital to rebuilding the area affected by the tsunami. Eventually, the Princess of Thailand offered her support for the education of migrant children, giving us hope that girls like Mi would be better protected while her parents were away at work. Instead of being vulnerable and alone, one day Burmese children would all be allowed to go to school alongside Thai children.

For me, however, the personal effects of the trip were ongoing.

No matter how hard I tried, I could not sleep. **How could I get on the plane and leave children like Mi behind?** What happened to the young boy watching the show on the border? I tossed and turned. There were no answers. I could not sleep—not for one night, then not for another. I took over-the-counter sleeping pills; they did not work.

After a third night without sleep, I felt delirious. I was unable to focus. I knocked on my neighbor's door. As luck would have it, she was a crisis counselor for diplomats serving overseas. I asked her, "Can you refer me to a counselor? I think I need to talk to someone."

When I got to see the counselor, *he asked me how many critical events I had experienced* as a relief worker. I told him about the car accident in South Africa and a co-worker, Ricardo's, death in Afghanistan. Yet, it was the abuse of Mi that really bothered me. In many ways, leaving her behind made me feel like I was abandoning myself.

"I can't believe I left her there defenseless," I told him.

The counselor encouraged me to accept that *suffering is part of the human condition.* He helped me see that I couldn't correct every injustice or protect every child. I had to accept the fact that I couldn't do more for little Mi.

To be honest, I wanted to adopt her and bring Mi home with me. But I never met her parents, and she probably didn't have a birth certificate. Plus, I was only 27 years old. I made just enough money to rent a one-bedroom apartment in the city. I didn't have a partner, and I wasn't ready to have a family yet. But still, the desire was there.

Ricardo

Talking with the counselor helped me get back to sleep. Once I got some rest, I began dreaming about another place. I had to come to terms with what happened in Afghanistan.

At the start of the Iraq War, the U.S. military requested that every humanitarian in the south of Afghanistan, all 20 of us, receive a mandatory security briefing. They instituted a mandatory *"stay in place"* policy for several days for all international personnel since insurgent activity was expected to pick up.

After three days of confinement, each agency gave their staff discretion about whether to travel beyond Kandahar. I held my teams back. Ricardo, my friend who was an engineer with the Red Cross, went to check on his wells. His vehicle came upon a group of terrorists affiliated with Al-Qaeda. They executed him in the desert. A high-level terrorist named Mullah Omar took responsibility for his death.

When they told me that Ricardo was dead, I couldn't believe it was true. Ricardo was the first volunteer from El Salvador to become an international delegate working overseas with the

International Committee of the Red Cross (ICRC). After realizing we both loved to salsa, we became good friends. He spoke to me in Spanish, even though I didn't speak the language. He would tell me,

"Sarah, I feel like you understand everything I say," as he laughed full heartedly.

Ricardo Munguia died several days after the Iraq War began. After he was executed, I was evacuated out of the area, traveling overland through the Turkmenistan border before reaching the United States.

I told the counselor about losing Ricardo and how devastating his traumatic death was for me. I saw his lifeless body after they brought him back from the desert. What I could not believe is that they also beat up his face. He had a jovial, round face that always made me laugh.

"I should have told him not to go," I said to the counselor. I knew it was too dangerous. I held my teams back, but he decided to go forward. He was a water and sanitation engineer. Kandahar province was a bone-dry desert where people were desperate for water. *"Still, I should have warned him,"* I insisted. The counselor looked straight at me and asked, sternly,

"Did you ever tell Ricardo what to do? He was an engineer. Did you tell him how to dig wells and what to do with the water they produced?"

"No," I said. *"I would never tell him what to do. He was excellent at his job."*

"There, you see," the counselor said. *"You would not have told him what to do.*

He made his own decision to go into the desert that day. You couldn't have known that he would be ambushed. You are not to blame."

The counselor was right. How could I blame myself for Ricardo's death? Was it possible to protect anyone under such circumstances? On one level, I accepted that no one was to blame. Still, the loss of this good friend and humanitarian cut deep. When I came home from Afghanistan, I would see people playing in the park and wonder,

How can anyone be happy? Don't they know there's a war going on?

It took a long time for me to recover. After Ricardo died, I thought the world would never be good again. One night, *he appeared to me in a dream.* I was sitting at a table, writing a letter to his family. I had re-written the letter several times, but I had not mailed it out yet. I wanted them to know how exceptional he was and about the great work he did right up until he died. Ricardo sat down at the table beside me, looked at me caringly, and said, *"Sarah, I am dead."*

I mailed the letter to Ricardo's family the next day. A weight had lifted off my shoulders and my heavy heart. With the help of the counselor and support from loving friends, eventually, gradually, the world become good again. I was finally able to accept the painful loss.

Traumatic Stress

Doing humanitarian work in crisis settings will come at a personal cost. It can cost you your life. You could be kidnapped or held hostage and violated in any number of ways, same as the people you are trying to help. Living and working in a conflict zone places you in the middle of a chaotic, unstable environment. Even the best agencies are unable to stop bad things from happening to you and those around you. You may lose your idealistic outlook about your purpose for being there. That is why you have to be prepared, as I mentioned earlier in the book. You also need a support network to see you through the dark days.

Prolonged exposure to human suffering, experiencing critical incidents, and witnessing violence can lead to trauma. When I stopped sleeping after the tsunami, this was an involuntary, traumatic response. I wanted to sleep, but I was unable to shut off part of my brain sending worried signals about things beyond my control. There is a science behind traumatic experiences that makes it difficult to simply deal with the response on your own.

When you have a traumatic incident, part of the cerebral cortex of the brain, called the hippocampus, is unable to process an overload of information, resulting in challenges to your cognitive functioning. Working through trauma requires being able to process what happened so you can place memories in context. When you can put these memories behind you, your brain adapts and puts them in their place, reducing the hyper-awareness you felt before. The process of healing is not just emotional but physical as well. Working with a trained therapist can help you determine that you are no longer responding to trauma but are on the road to recovery.

You can also experience vicarious trauma based on something that happens to another person—by bearing witness to suffering. Being in the field and working in crisis can also expose you to danger that is completely random, such as the car accident I survived in South Africa.

When you go to help people in harm's way, you might find yourself in danger also. It is normal to have a fearful response to dangerous situations and to experience this fear vicariously through helping others. Knowing the challenges that you will face in any crisis will help you to be better prepared.

When your work involves helping people, you also need to take good care of yourself. It's important to take the time to debrief and share your experience. When something bad happens, your body and your brain need time to recover. You may need to take a break between deployments and make more time for leisure and personal relationships.

Taking time for yourself and your recovery is not a sign of weakness. It is a sign of strength.

Having a strong support network of friends and family was key to my personal recovery. There were days, especially in between assignments, when I wondered how I would ever get myself together. I want to share with you that things do fall in place, time and time again. Struggling with difficult memories may require you to pause, but you will eventually recover and continue on your way. Recovery is within reach. Give yourself time to heal.

I don't want you to get discouraged by reports of bad things that happen in the world or by the difficult things that happen as you do good work. However, I do want you to have a realistic idea about what you're up against. Here's my quick take on how to manage hard times:

1. Remember that there are **real threats to your safety** and determined perpetrators of violence, not imaginary ones, wreaking havoc in the world. These include individuals and armed groups that persecute people

based on their identity and who violate the physical integrity of people by committing acts of violence. There are leaders who use war and conflict for their personal gain. As a humanitarian, the closer you get to affected people and the root cause of the problem, the more familiar you will become with these perpetrators of violence. These same actors have the ability to harm you and stop your work. **Acknowledge this reality and remain vigilant about your personal safety.**

2. Obstacles to your health and well-being are also **a real and present danger.** You may get sick, contract a disease, or get in a road accident. Random acts and unforeseen events may have a significant impact on your ability to function and complete the work you set out to do. These obstacles are real and have to be managed.

   You may need to take time out for healing and recovery. You may get evacuated from your area of operations, or you may have to stop work for a number of other reasons. To manage this, you have to remain flexible to changing circumstances. You also have to be vigilant about your health and have a plan for self-care to maintain your wellness.

3. When you face a dark night, a traumatic incident, or critical event, **know that you will recover.** Get help by debriefing with a trained therapist. Seek guidance from colleagues who have been through traumatic incidents. Don't be afraid of reaching out to family and friends to share your experience. Letting people help you is key to your recovery. After giving so much to other people, you need to be willing to receive care

from others. This can be a humbling experience for people who are capable and experienced helpers.

4. **Take good care of yourself.** Be patient with your own recovery. You know what you need more than anyone else. When you feel down or are physically constrained, you need to take the time to recover. It's important to be in good physical and mental shape before going on assignment again. Every time I get on a plane, I think about the announcement:

"In the event of an emergency, put your own oxygen mask on before assisting others."

Remember; the greatest gift you can give the world is to offer yourself. The time and skills you cultivate to address the problems you see in the world are your greatest asset. You are making a difference in individual lives and in very complex situations. Oftentimes, the problems you face are beyond your control. Your ability to accept the world as it is rather than the world as it should be can also help you manage expectations of yourself and the limits of your organization to fix particular problems. When you feel that conditions are out of control, it's important to regain a sense of personal direction over what you can control. It's also important to take time to rest and do things that you enjoy, such as spending time with the people you love.

When you accept your own limits, you can appreciate at a deeper level what is possible. *You can better empathize with people who have experienced pain and loss because you, too, have suffered these things.* Then, you can move forward and take the next step on your journey.

11

FINDING YOUR PEOPLE

Life Choices

In my twenties and thirties, I was always striving to do more and to diversify my work so that I would not get bored. I wanted to experience everything the world had to offer. I did not want to settle down or slow down. But then, major events changed my course. The car accident in South Africa and losing Ricardo in Afghanistan forced me to stop and think about what I was doing and why I was doing this work.

Everyone kept telling me how to climb the ladder of the organization where I worked, how to make more money, and how to get a better job title to get ahead. But I had to figure out how I could keep on doing this work and stay alive.

During those times of transition, and also in between assignments, I questioned my life and career choices. I asked myself:

Should I have chosen a more financially lucrative career that would allow me to have a nicer car, a bigger home, a more robust savings account, and a better retirement?

Should I have stayed in one place longer and climbed the career ladder? Was I too impatient, too impulsive, too driven in my work? Should I have chosen a safer life path?

Somewhere in the back of your mind, doubts like this can travel along with you, eroding confidence. No matter what choices you make, every few years it's a good idea to take a step back and think about the path you have chosen.

Why did you go this way? Is there another path you should be on? What road should you take next? You are only one person, and you will have to make choices. Even though many paths are laid out before you, you cannot do everything. You will have to choose a path, and often times those directional choices are not easy.

Gaining Perspective

Flying on an airplane always gives me perspective about my life and choices. As the aircraft rises above the clouds, a bright horizon is revealed. If only it were that easy to rise above our struggles and big life questions—but more often than not, it's hard to see the "bright horizon" ahead.

How do you maintain perspective when you want to move forward, but you feel set back? What do you do when you question your life or career path and you cannot see the road ahead? What do you do when life starts to overwhelm you?

I highly recommend that you purposefully **build a support network of trusted mentors and friends** to help you all along the way. In this chapter, we will explore how to build such a network.

When you are in a helping profession, giving yourself to others on a daily basis, you need personal relationships in your life that help you rest, play, and enjoy life. **Having a "tribe" of supportive people will help re-charge your batteries when things get tough.**

Some people have a tight-knit family network and others do not. I envy families that live close enough to one another to have family meals and regular get-togethers beyond the usual holiday gatherings.

If you are working in a large city or regional hub, however, it's likely that your family lives far away. In this case, it's important to have friends who are like family—to find your tribe. Especially if you continue to travel for work and are coming in and out of town, you need to come back to people you can count on. This is a key factor of personal happiness in a professional world where people rely on their planners to schedule every minute of their day—and their weekends too.

What a gift it is to have people in your life you can call at any time, people you can see without making a scheduled appointment. We all need friends who are like family. Find those friends and be that friend to someone else.

It's not easy to find your tribe in every location where you live or work, though—especially if you are living in a different culture where people speak another language. However, there are a few ways to find and identify people with whom you can establish a tighter bond of friendship.

Here are a few pieces of advice that have helped me find my tribe:

1. **Put yourself out there**—go to social events such as dinners, parties, clubs, meet ups, churches, gyms, and exercise groups. Go to places where you can find people with similar interests. Even when you don't feel like getting out, when you would rather stay in, *go meet people!*

2. **Have meaningful conversations**—ask people questions about their lives, families, experiences, and beliefs. If you keep the conversation light, you may never know

whether the person shares common interests and values. Be willing to go deeper to find your tribe.

3. **Be invitational**—once you meet someone or a group of people you like, invite them into your space. Whether that space is your home or other places you like to go regularly, make them feel like they are important to you by showing openness, generosity, and kindness.

4. **Be helpful**—close friends share a common interest in helping one another, whether that's picking up a child from school, picking up something you need at the store, or getting your mail while you're away, etc. Be helpful to people you would like to be friends with, and they are likely to return the favor, showing their sincere support.

These are some common ways I have found my tribe wherever I go. Yet, every culture has its own way of showing friendship. For example, in parts of West Africa people show they are friends by taking one another's belongings and then returning them—the most common item being shoes. In Senegal, people do not wear shoes inside the home. Instead, they leave them at the door. When you leave a home, taking someone else's shoes is a compliment. It shows you intend to return them to the owner by paying that person a visit—and that you are literally willing to *"walk in their shoes."*

People in your tribe must have another essential quality—they must be people who care about you in a time of need. As a humanitarian, you are busy caring for the needs of others. But close friends care for one another too. If you get sick, who would you want to be there for you? Your tribe is made up of friends you want beside you when things go wrong, not just friends with whom you party on the weekend.

How do you know if someone is part of your tribe? They are there for you when you need them, without having to set aside the time or make an appointment. Your tribe shares common attributes which makes them like family, helping and supporting one another—within reason. You do not have to be your best self to keep these friendships. You can have a bad day or be gone for a while and pick back up where you left things.

Everyone needs a tribe. Get to know people and become known. Allow yourself to love others and to be loved. Find a good friend, be a good friend, and all will be well with you.

Note on Compound Living

In the humanitarian sector, particularly in austere conditions, it is likely that some of you will live in a house or compound with your colleagues. Your lodging could be in a shipping container converted into a small room. You could live in the same location where you get up and go to work, right next door, in a containerized office. This type of working environment creates especially close living conditions that make it hard to separate your personal space from your professional life. You will come to know everything about people in such conditions, perhaps even more than you want to know or should know.

My advice to you about these conditions is to guard your privacy and the privacy of others. You will see these people again as you progress in your career. Maintain your personal integrity by living in such a way that your future professional reputation depends on it. Having integrity means making decisions that can withstand public scrutiny. This is incredibly challenging, particularly in war zones and remote areas where people feel there is no accountability for their personal behavior. However, people with long careers in the same field remember everything. Make sure that what people remember about you is good, and if any negative incidents happen, make sure to address them right away.

Your Professional Network

As much as a tribe supports your personal life, cultivating a professional network is essential to your career. But it's important not to confuse the two, as some people do. Someone who is important to your professional network is a respected colleague with whom you should cultivate a working relationship. This is a person with whom you are going to have to schedule calls or meetings according to other work priorities.

Building your professional network takes time and intentionality. You should carefully consider, at each stage of your career, who you need to know to accomplish the work at hand. There will also be people whom you would like to get to know based on shared interests and goals.

Your Supervisor

The most important person to build your professional relationship with is your immediate supervisor. Your boss will play a key role in working with you to address your performance, which will include pointing out areas where you excel and areas for further growth. Regularly seek out feedback from your boss and other senior colleagues so that you are aware of what is required of you.

One of the toughest situations to be in is when you do not know what success looks like in a given role. Make sure you ask your supervisor what will make you successful in the role. Also ask if your boss prefers a certain communication style or schedule of meetings that you should keep in mind. Paying attention to what your supervisor wants and keeping open communication will help you excel in your work and address any issues that come up.

Take a Genuine Interest in People

In order to build a strong professional network within and outside your organization, you have to take a genuine interest in people. This means taking an interest not only in their job title or accomplishments but also learning from their experience. This means asking people questions about themselves and why they chose a particular career path.

Ultimately, you are trying to form professional friendships that will be important alliances in reaching the greater goals you set out to accomplish. This means you will need multiple interactions with colleagues to build on these important relationships.

But first, you have to meet people who are key stakeholders in your career field. If you choose a humanitarian career, you will also have to pick a specialty area within a specific emergency response sector. For every sector, such as food aid, shelter, health, or child protection, there are leaders at various levels in a number of key locations:

Global Cluster Leads

The Office for the Coordination of Humanitarian Affairs (OCHA) manages a list of global leads for each sector of response. Sometimes these leads are within a United Nations agency, and some of them are within respected nongovern-mental organizations (NGOs) that partner with the UN lead agency. These leaders tend to be at agency headquarters in New York, Geneva, London, and Washington, D.C., among other locations.

The best way to meet leaders in these organizations is by hearing them speak at major events, conferences, or online forums. Sometimes these meetings are open to the public, other times you will need special permission to attend. Many large international meetings also accept short-term volunteers, giving you a backstage pass to the forum. Use these opportunities to ask a question at the forum, and give your business card to the speakers afterward, asking if you can send them a follow-up email. If you want to reach out to a senior leader, you will need to reach their personal assistant to request a call or meeting. You can also follow them on social media and LinkedIn to find out more about their work.

Regional Geographic Hubs

Relief agencies have regional geographic hubs on each con-tinent that coordinate humanitarian response. Senior leaders of UN agencies and NGOs also operate around major hubs, including Nairobi, Bangkok, Amman, Cairo, and San Jose, among others. Meeting regional leaders is a matter of prox-imity; if you are located in a regional hub, become part of inter-agency working groups and attend forums within your community of interest. Socialize among people in your field and ask colleagues for introductions.

Where You Are

If you do not live in a major hub for international work, you can also identify leaders right where you are in the nonprofit and charitable sector that may have connections overseas. Look for professional associations, donors, foundations, and academic institutions with international connections that are close by. Also, find ways to get involved by traveling to regional or headquarter meetings, and participating in virtual conferences. Read major reports from leaders in your chosen field, follow these leaders on social media, and make your own contributions by sharing interesting content and research in the field.

Networking Do's and Don'ts

Remember that someone who considers themselves to be important, including anyone who holds a senior position in any organization, has limited time to network with you. This is because that person also has a boss, board, donor, or committee to whom s/he also answers. That person has a work plan with deadlines, hundreds of emails to return, and dozens of meetings on any given day.

How do you get someone to be in your professional network? I receive dozens of requests every month to meet with someone for coffee or review their resume for a job. Due to my work and travel schedule, it is not possible to see each person individually. Here are some basic tips for networking the right way:

Networking *Do's*
- Do have a clear ask—do you want the person to introduce you to someone, review your resume, or help you get a specific job? The more generic the request, the less likely the person is to answer. The more succinct your request is, the greater likelihood of a reply.

- Do come recommended—get someone who knows the person in question to introduce you.
- Do try to meet in person—try to get face time with the individual. Make a good first impression.
- Do have your resume prepared—make sure it's a good, clean copy before you ask someone to review it. Also, have a short writing sample that is relevant to your field or sector.

Networking *Don'ts*

- Don't ask someone for multiple favors—a student once sent me a list of ten organizations she would like to work for, asking for contacts in each one. I told her to choose one of them so I could introduce her to one person.
- Don't take too much of a person's time—30 minutes should be enough. Don't ask the person to take an hour or more out of a busy day. Today, many busy people reject requests for coffee and take calls or virtual meetings instead.
- Don't forget to send a thank you note—I always remember the people who thank me for my time, and I often forget those who do not.
- Don't appear overly selfish—be curious and ask questions. Ask potential mentors about their work and current projects.

Managing Transition

One of the challenges in any career track is managing transitions. Whether you're just starting out in your career or you're wondering whether to change course, you will be able to manage transitions if you cultivate the personal and professional relationships that can help you discern your next steps.

Many relief workers just starting out receive short-term contracts for three, six, or twelve months. This is a short period of time to accomplish a great deal of work. This means you are giving your all to an organization that can only guarantee you a short-term contract. Organizations let out these short-term contracts for numerous reasons. Sometimes they are testing your ability, other times it is due to insufficient funding for a permanent post. Although you can make good money on a short-term assignment once you have the required technical skills, you will eventually need predictable income over time. The best way to get a full-time position is to lean on your professional network to help you find a permanent placement.

Returning Home

For aid workers coming back from overseas, returning home presents its own challenges. Re-entry can be tough if you don't have a supportive tribe in place that understands what you did overseas. It's important to share your experiences with friends and to have patience with family members who might not understand. You will also need to save money so you can pay bills in-between assignments and take a break when you need it. It's also important to consider investing in property so you have your own home to return to and to consider the timeframe of when and if you would like to "settle down" or have a family.

Your Life Choices

At times in my career, I faced tough choices about what to do next. When my path seemed uncertain, I had to step back, reconsider my role in the world, and lean on friends and colleagues to help me see the next step. **While you will make many** decisions about your life as an individual, you also need a support network to help you get where you want to go.

When you see many paths ahead, the decisions you make about where to go next will include family, health, and financial considerations. There may be times in your career when you have to change course. For humanitarians who want to have children or who need to care for aging parents, these are pivot points when you may need to live in a stable place. This can be a hard transition for people who have spent many years in the field and are not used to working in an office setting.

Becoming restless with "normal life" is a hazard for emergency responders. Cultivating deep personal relationships can make all the difference to accepting life changes. The alternative is to live in tension with yourself and to have unrealistic expectations of other people. During times of transition, set realistic goals and rely on the support of family and friends.

Remember; even if you change career fields altogether, if you choose to become a banker or a dentist, you can still be a humanitarian. You can live in solidarity with those who are suffering in many ways.

You do not have to choose a linear path. Make your own way, a way that reflects your unique contribution. With the right support, you can bring all that you have to offer, at any age and every stage of life, to make your work a success.

12

LIVING YOUR BEST LIFE

"People who say it cannot be done should
not interrupt those who are doing it."
George Bernard Shaw

Your Individual Path

As you can see from reading this book, my path has taken me to many places. To live your best life, a life that serves others, you will take your own, individual path.

I started out working for the U.S. Senate, which authorizes funding for emergency relief programs, as well as military expenditures. Some people believe the U.S. Government is the most dynamic influencer of humanitarian action in the world. However, when compared with other nations worldwide, members of the European Union (EU) and the Nordic countries make up a larger amount of contributions.

Yet, even the sum total of all humanitarian expenditure globally, estimated at $27 billion annually, is not enough to resolve all the problems facing the world.[36] This is because, as I have mentioned, the root causes of a crisis are complex. They are deeply entrenched in social, economic, and political

---

[36]See the Global Humanitarian Assistance Report 2018 produced by Development Initiatives, and the UN Financial Tracking Service (FTS) for more information on official humanitarian expenditure.

realities that require good governance at the national and local level.

A Road Less Traveled

My career path was not linear. I did not climb ladders, trying to up my status in any one organization. Instead, I took an individual path based on my own perception of where I could make the most difference at the time. I went from working in the Senate to working for a large NGO, getting a graduate degree, then managing a United Nations program, working for the International Committee of the Red Cross, forming a network of experts to improve the protection of people, then advising NATO and the U.S. military on complex operations.

Occasionally, I wonder what my life would be like had I climbed a traditional ladder of success. Would I be a senior leader in a respected international organization? Would I have a notable position in government? Perhaps.

As I reflect on all these experiences, I am happy with the path I chose for my life. I am happy—not because I achieved everything I set out to do. There is still more. There are more things I would like to do. There is more work that needs to be done.

I am happy because I have lived my best life by helping people. Living in solidarity and in service to others is deeply rewarding. Seeing the extent to which my work has contributed to the safety of people in danger, I am satisfied knowing that *I gave people a chance to see another day*. I want to see each and every person, including you, live a full life. Doing the work of serving humanity, in turn, makes me feel fully alive.

My hope is that this book has inspired you to help humanity. I want you to have the assurance that your

education and experience are preparing you to live the life of your dreams. Helping people won't always be easy, but it will always be rewarding.

Today, being a humanitarian and helping humanity could mean taking an entirely new approach. Yes, international agencies need more workers to go out into the field, but they also need more funding to get them there.

Yet, we could also use a better way of life, a way of caring for the needs of one another, to take hold among the people of all nations. We could use a common belief in the worth and dignity of all people regardless of gender, race, religion, nationality, political opinion, sexual preference, or social group. We need more people who care for nature and the environment that sustains life.

You Are Needed

You can "be" and "do" many things to contribute to a better world. You could become a climate scientist and prevent natural disasters by mitigating the risk of extreme weather patterns.

The world needs environmentalists to plant trees and clean up waste and lobby for environmental protection. You can help people live healthier, more sustainable lives.

You could invent new technologies so people who speak different languages can communicate better across geographic boundaries.

The world needs people who understand big data to study patterns of violence in order to improve early warning and make the outbreak of conflict more predictable.

Facts matter—however inconvenient they are. You could work in social media and journalism, bearing witness by clearly speaking and writing the truth.

You could be a doctor, public health specialist, or epidemiologist tracking the outbreak of epidemics and curing diseases.

You can also be a student, a parent, or a concerned citizen who uses your voice to uplift others within your community.

You can also be an accountant, artist, business owner, engineer, lawyer, teacher, or social worker and be involved in service projects in numerous ways. You can volunteer in your spare time and serve on the board of charitable organizations.

Helpers are ordinary people who do extraordinary things. They are ready to act when the need arises, wherever they happen to be in the world.

The world needs more leaders who care about people and are accountable for their actions. You could run for office and be a political leader. We need leaders at every level of government to look out for the needs of people.

By working for the diplomatic corps or foreign service, you can bring clarity to international relations. You can help create conditions for peace and prosperity that bring about an end to conflict.

The humanitarian sector also needs people in business and finance to overcome gaps in funding and to offer refugees jobs instead of handouts so they can live a dignified life, becoming self-reliant and meeting their own needs.

The world needs more people to make their way from the sidelines of life to center stage. It needs more people participating in the political process and the global economy. It needs people who are dedicated to social progress that are equally committed to pursuing justice and equality.

In the course of my work, I meet a few thousand people every year. Each month, I collect hundreds of business cards from people I meet at different conferences and working groups. I have too many business cards for a rolodex. I keep a master spreadsheet with tens of thousands of names. It's hard to remember all those names, so I organize the cards in binders, reminding me of when and where I met each group of people. There are sections for U.S. and foreign government officials, United Nations agencies, and nongovernmental organizations (NGOs), as well as prominent individuals, such as donors not affiliated with any entity.

The humanitarian life is not an anonymous one. You will need to know many people in order to be successful in this work. But this work is not about making a name for yourself.

The names of the most important people I have met are not in the binders. They don't even have business cards. Many of them do not have an address or a computer to check their email. Some of them cannot read or write. These are the people whose faces, rather than their names, have left an indelible mark on me. These are the people whose lives are changed by responding to the call to serve others—the beneficiaries who have survived against overwhelming odds and the courageous aid workers who selflessly work to assist and protect them.

Nor am I famous. Many of the people I have helped do not know my name. The groups of people who I advocated for with governments, the refugees who needed a home, the men thrown in prison and persecuted for their political activity, the women suffering from violence, the children who lacked an education—many of them do not know my name. They never will.

Living a life of service is not about becoming famous. It is not about your personal success *per se*. It is about what you can do for others. Helping others may earn you a good reputation, but that won't be your reward.

Your reward will be seeing people and places that were once in crisis transformed by the changes you made possible. The return to normalcy will be so mundane that only those who lived through the crisis there will know the changes that have taken place—but you will see a place and know that it is not the same because of what you did there.

The people you met, who were once living in hardship, have found a new life. Some of them will have passed away, which is the natural order of things. Yet, thousands of them will be in safer places, living healthier lives with the resources to set the course of their own future. Their success is your success. Their story is your story. Because of them, you will never be the same.

The people you meet will change you as a person. They will show you true generosity and real friendship, and they will give you the gift of a life well-lived. They will show you what it means to be fully human, in any circumstance. The people I met in refugee camps and border towns, during a disaster, and in the aftermath of tragedy changed my life. The individuals whose lives touched mine are men and women like Chuck (the man who could not read in Maine); Gladys (the cleaning lady overlooked in Washington D.C.); Mrs. Dang (a refugee beaten by her husband in Manila); little Mi (who was abused in the slums of Phuket); the woman whose breast we sewed back on at a hospital in Soweto; the women in New Orleans who got right in my face, asking for help; and the naked men who came up to me asking where they could find clothes. From the people of Louisiana to the widow in Afghanistan; and the countless aid workers like Ricardo who risk their lives to help people in distress, each person has taught me what life is all about.

Each individual story pointed me to many other people living in similar circumstances. I think of each one of them every time I am called to help someone because each circumstance made me more capable of responding to people's unique needs. By directing help their way, bringing attention to their situation, I was changed. I became a better person by living in solidarity with them and by smiling upon their successes, however small, each time I was able to change a life.

Each person taught me to do whatever I could, one step at a time. When I would meet with refugees in far off camps, they would always ask me the same thing:

"Please tell my story," they would say over and over again.

"If people knew my story, they wouldn't allow these things to happen anymore."

People who are suffering in silence, at this very moment, believe that if we could hear their cries for help, we would not turn away. If we knew their stories, if we could see their faces, would we let war destroy their homes and tear their families apart?

No; if we could see them, we would respond to their thirst for water and hunger for food. We would see to it that they had what they needed.

If we could see them, things would change. We would change. We would all be humanitarians.

Stories showing how people survive overwhelming odds inspire us. They move us to help the next person we see, then the next person, so we keep passing on goodwill. They call us to action, to live a life beyond borders and beyond ourselves.

This urgency of passing on stories is also palpable among survivors of the Holocaust, when six million Jewish people were killed in Europe. Yet, over three million people survived this horrific atrocity.

As a student, I was fascinated by these tales of survival, reading as many survivor accounts as I could. I wanted to know: how did they make it? What kept them going? I learned from my favorite author, Victor Frankl, who survived Auschwitz despite losing most of his family members, that the will to live was based on the desire to care for others.

"We who lived in concentration camps can remember the men who walked through the huts comforting others, giving away their last piece of bread. They may have been few in number, but they offer sufficient proof that everything can be taken from a man but one thing: the last of the human freedoms-to choose one's attitude in any given set of circumstances, to choose one's own way."

Victor Frankl, Holocaust survivor

Every day offers us an opportunity to save lives. Every survivor who has lived through war, who makes it through a catastrophic disaster, contributes toward human progress. They can help ensure that we do not look away next time we see bad things happening in the world. They give us hope and provide meaning to the words that we will "never again" allow for the targeted killing and untimely death of our fellow man, woman, and child.

Every Life is Worth Saving

What we are aiming to achieve by our work is allowing each person to live as fully as they possibly can so they can make their own unique contribution to the world.

We are bound together by the story of human progress. Every idea and invention that has ever changed the world is something that brings people together and benefits us collectively. Planes, automobiles, the internet, and mobile phones—technology has brought people together—rather than dividing us apart. Inventions in science and medicine have resulted in the opportunity for people to live longer lives and in the ability to treat diseases that were once considered fatal. Philosophies like representative government are expanding the reach of democracy. Legal reforms are bringing nations into alignment on human rights and gender equality. Business practices are rooting out corruption and strengthening supply chain mechanisms, ensuring fairness to workers who make items we consume.

Every time we lose a life to unnecessary suffering, we are missing a piece of human history. We are missing out on the contribution that person could have made to humanity as a whole. This is the hope of humanity: that by coming together, we are greater than the forces that seek to tear us apart and that together, we can find solutions to the world's toughest problems.

This is how we know that the little things we do each day are making a difference—by believing that our lives are part of a bigger picture. By actively being part of the solution to the problems we see, it gives us faith that *we can overcome evil with good, achieve equal rights for all people, and bring light to dark places*. Passing on this hope is a great gift. It is a gift you can freely give to anyone, whether you are caring for your friends and neighbors close to home or helping people overseas.

One of my greatest life lessons is the importance of living in the moment and taking the time to be available to people. Even if you do great work to feed the hungry and clothe the naked, no amount of money you can program will help more than what you do, every day of your life, with the resources you have, wherever you are at this very moment in your life.

From the moment I came into the world, the village where I was born hoped that I would bring them one thing: rain. They wanted an end to the drought that made them hungry and kept them in need. Living a life of service and helping humanity in crisis has taught me that if you cannot bring rain, then bring the next best thing—yourself. Offer yourself to the problems you see and work with people who are dedicated to finding solutions. Your unique gifts are what the world needs.

Be available where you are now. Be ready to respond to the needs you see in the world, and you will do great things for humanity. Strength and courage to you on your journey. Go forward and live your best life.

The world needs you.

Epilogue

This book reflects the lessons I learned in the field as a humanitarian relief worker. Today, my work involves analyzing patterns of violence, assessing who is at-risk, and advising military operations about protecting civilians. This includes analyzing ways to prevent all types of violence, including the targeting of minorities, taking of children to be child soldiers, taking of women and girls as sex slaves, reducing civilian deaths, and stopping atrocities such as ethnic conflict and genocide.

I've had the good fortune of working with many nations, including the United States and partner militaries within the North Atlantic Treaty Organization (NATO), to set a higher standard for the protection of civilians in conflict. The views expressed in this book are my own and do not reflect any government office or agency.

Whether I am advising a coalition of nations about a complex operation or a humanitarian agency about a particular problem, the stories in this book have influenced every word of advice I have to offer. If we are a product of our experiences, then I am intrinsically linked to every person who has shown me humanity at its best—and at its worst. I am also shaped by friends and colleagues who are dedicated to bringing about the best in humanity.

I have found this love for humanity to be my greatest calling and purpose in life. It is worth dedicating your life's work to this end. If we do not help one another live well, we will die poorly. There is no need to see the world suffer as it does and then do nothing about it. In this book, I have described the many things you can do and the vision that you can accomplish as you go forth and do good work.

I pass the baton to you—

Sarah

ACKNOWLEDGEMENTS

I would like to thank God for being with me every step of the journey and for all the traveling mercies I have received along the way. Thank you to every friend, colleague, and companion that has lived this humanitarian life with me. I am truly grateful for your comradery and your friendship.

Thank you to my loving family, especially my Mom, for giving me a heart of compassion to help others, and my brother Caleb and his wife Julie, who embody a life of service to their community. Thank you to my niece and nephew Jane and Joe for being awesome. I know you will do great things!

Thanks to all my family in Maine and to the wonderful people of Maine who inspired me to serve others, including friends from First Baptist Church and colleagues in the Office of U.S. Senator Olympia Snowe. Thanks also to my Gordon College friends who are like family to me!

Thank you to my literary team, including my agent Lisa Jackson, fellow author Lisa Jo Baker, my writing coach David Hazard, and the team at *Tremendous Leadership,* including Dr. Tracey Jones, Leah Hess, and Tim Schulte, as well as *Variance Author Services* and Adi Leigh Brown.

Thank you to my colleagues at the U.S. Army Peacekeeping and Stability Operations Institute (PKSOI) who supported my time and effort on this book at the U.S. Army War College, especially to Dr. Karen Finkenbinder, Colonel Ryan Wolfgram, Colonel (Ret.) Brian Foster, Colonel (Ret.) Dwight Raymond, Colonel Scot Storey, Mr. John Stepanksy, and Mr. George

McDonnell for your encouragement. Thanks also to the Prairie Quest team.

Thank you to all the early readers and friends who helped refine the book including Sid Balman, Jason Boxt, Andrea Britton, Dale Hanson Bourke, Lindsay Musser Hough, Stacey Winston Kohli, Dulce Magloire, Luz Martinez, Joan Maruskin, Abi Riak, Joseph Tompkins, Hoi Trinh, Jen Tynan-Tyrrell, Linda Wilkinson, and Patrick Kennedy. Thanks also to the Around the World Book Club, including Jean Poole, Carol Wasserman, Katherine Cassidy, and Katherine Klos for being early readers.

Thank you to faculty and students at Dickinson College who reviewed the book including Dr. Gary Kirk, Dr. Missy Niblock, Abby Kaija, Mallorey Fitzgerald, Ava Larson, and Christian Merino Rubio. Thanks to faculty and students at Messiah College including Dr. Jenell Paris, Anastasia Couch, Hannah Domaracki, and Ruben Langston Smith.

Thank you to my colleagues working tirelessly to help refugees at the U.S. Committee for Refugees and Immigrants, Lutheran Immigration and Refugee Service, Refugees International, World Vision, the United Nations Foundation, the UN High Commissioner for Refugees, the International Organization for Migration, and other humanitarian organizations. Thanks also to the Refugee Studies Center at Oxford University for preparing me for this field. Special thanks to Daryl Byler, Dr. Beth Ferris, Jacob Kurtzer, Doug Mercado, Anne Richard, and Eric Schwartz for reviewing the book.

Thanks to everyone I have worked with on the protection of civilians, including the NATO Concept Development and Experimentation Group at Allied Command Transformation; SHAPE; the Human Security Unit; and colleagues from

Canada, Finland, France, Ireland, Italy, the Netherlands, Norway, and the United Kingdom. Thanks also to friends at the International Committee of the Red Cross, the Center for Civilians in Conflict, and the Stimson Center who have advanced the protection of civilians in crisis.

Thanks to everyone who supported Protect the People while it was an operational organization, especially those who served on the Board of Directors including Royce Murray, Chuck Keefe, Jolynn Shoemaker, Anita Bhatt, and Michael Clemens. Special thanks to Sidley Austin LLP and Renner and Company CPA for supporting this work.

Thanks to my friends in Alexandria, Virginia, and Washington, D.C. who cheered for me all along the way, including an amazing "tribe" of women, my CrossFit group, Clay Williamson, and friends at Washington Community Fellowship and Aldersgate United Methodist Church.

Thanks to the people of Afghanistan, Haiti, Kenya, the Philippines, Sierra Leone, South Africa, Switzerland, Thailand, Ukraine, Vietnam, and more places where I had the pleasure to work and live and get to know you.

Above all else, thank you for reading this book. Thank you for making the world a better place. Now, it is time for you to write your story.

Onward!

Author's Note
THANK YOU FOR READING!

Dear Reader,

Thank you for reading *Bring Rain.* If you loved the book and have a minute to spare, I would really appreciate a short review on the page or site where you bought the book. Your help in spreading the word is greatly appreciated.

Reviews from readers like you make a huge difference to helping new readers find stories similar to *Bring Rain.*

Thanks for being who you are, and all that you do!
Sarah

P.S. Want me to speak to your organization, class, or book club?

Get in touch with me through my website at:
www.sarahpetrin.com

CPSIA information can be obtained
at www.ICGtesting.com
Printed in the USA
LVHW081636290721
694062LV00011B/133/J

9 781949 033472